Python for Web Hackers

Mastering Black Hat Techniques

Jason Bourny

Disclaimer

The information contained in this book, "**Python for Web Hackers: Mastering Black Hat Techniques**" by **Jason Bourny**, is provided for educational and informational purposes only. The content is technical in nature and is intended to enhance your understanding of cybersecurity, ethical hacking, and related topics.

Other books in the Python for Hackers series

"Python for Wireless Hacking: Exploiting Wi-Fi Networks and Bluetooth Devices"

"Advanced Python Scripting for Kali Linux: Exploiting Security Weaknesses"

"Python for Cryptography and Steganography: Concealing and Revealing Secrets"

"Python for OSINT: Tracking and Profiling Targets"

" Python IoT Infiltration: Hacking Internet of Things Devices"

" Python for Smartphone Hacking: Mobile Intrusions"

"Python for Browser Hackers: Attack and Exploit Vulnerabilities on the Web"

"Infernal Python Botnets Hackers: Building and Controlling Networks of Infected Devices"

For more information, or to book an event, contact :
(Email & Website)

Book design by Jason Bourny
Cover design by Jason Bourny

Introduction

Welcome to "**Python for Web Hackers: Mastering Black Hat Techniques**," a comprehensive guide that will transform the way you approach web security and hacking. Whether you're a seasoned penetration tester, a curious student, or a Python programming enthusiast, this book is your gateway to mastering the dark arts of web exploitation with one of the most powerful programming languages at your disposal: Python.

In today's digital landscape, the battleground for security is constantly evolving. Web applications, the lifeblood of modern online services, are perpetually under threat from attackers seeking to exploit vulnerabilities for their gain. This book dives deep into the world of web hacking, revealing the techniques and strategies employed by both black hat and ethical hackers to expose and fortify these weaknesses.

Our journey begins with the fundamentals, exploring the notorious SQL injection—a critical vulnerability that can bring entire databases to their knees. We'll dissect the mechanics of SQL injection, equipping you with Python scripts that automate the process of identifying and exploiting these vulnerabilities with precision and efficiency.

Next, we'll venture into the realm of cross-site scripting (XSS), another potent attack vector that targets the client-side of web applications. Through detailed examples and advanced Python coding, you'll learn how to craft XSS payloads that bypass even the most stringent security measures, giving you the edge in understanding and mitigating these threats.

But that's just the beginning. As we progress, we'll delve into a multitude of other vulnerabilities, teaching you how to exploit and defend against them. From session hijacking to parameter tampering, you'll gain a holistic understanding of web application security, all while honing your Python programming skills to automate and enhance your hacking endeavors.

This book is not just a collection of techniques—it's a call to arms for the next generation of cybersecurity warriors. The knowledge you acquire here will empower you to think like an attacker, anticipate their moves, and develop robust defenses. It's about transforming raw technical skills into a powerful toolkit for both offensive and defensive security.

So, are you ready to embark on this journey? To dive into the code, dissect vulnerabilities, and emerge as a master of Python-powered web hacking? Turn the page, and let's begin the adventure together. Your path to mastering black hat techniques starts here.

Chapter 1: Python for Web Hackers

Python is a versatile programming language that has gained immense popularity in recent years, especially among web hackers. With its simple syntax and powerful libraries, Python has become the go-to language for developing web applications, automating tasks, and even hacking into systems.

In this guide, we will provide an introduction to Python for web hackers, covering the basics of the language and how it can be used for various hacking purposes. Whether you are a beginner looking to learn Python for the first time or an experienced hacker looking to expand your skills, this guide will provide you with the knowledge you need to get started.

Python is a high-level, interpreted language that is known for its readability and ease of use. It is often compared to other programming languages like Java and C++, but it stands out for its simplicity and flexibility. Python uses indentation to define code blocks, making it easy to read and understand, even for beginners.

One of the key features of Python is its extensive standard library, which includes modules for a wide range of tasks, from web development to data analysis. This makes Python a powerful tool for hackers, as it allows them to quickly and easily write scripts to automate tasks or exploit vulnerabilities.

Python is also highly extensible, with a large number of third-party libraries available for a wide range of purposes. This allows hackers to leverage existing code and tools to speed up their development process and make their hacks more effective.

In addition to its versatility and ease of use, Python is also known for its security features. The language has built-in support for encryption, hashing, and other security protocols, making it a popular choice for developing secure applications and tools.

Python is often used in combination with other tools and languages, such as SQL, JavaScript, and HTML, to create dynamic web applications. Python's simplicity and flexibility make it easy to integrate with other technologies, allowing hackers to build complex systems that can interact with databases, APIs, and other web services.

One of the key advantages of Python for web hackers is its support for web frameworks, such as Django and Flask. These frameworks provide a set of tools and libraries for building web applications, making it easy to create interactive websites and web services.

Django, for example, is a popular web framework that follows the Model-View-Controller (MVC) architecture, making it easy to separate the different components of a web application. Flask, on the other hand, is a lightweight framework that is easy to set up and use, making it ideal for small projects and prototypes.

In addition to web frameworks, Python also supports a wide range of tools for web scraping, data analysis, and network programming. These tools allow hackers to gather information from websites, analyze data, and communicate with other systems over the internet.

Python's flexibility and extensibility make it a powerful tool for web hackers, allowing them to quickly prototype ideas, automate tasks, and exploit vulnerabilities. Whether you are a beginner looking to learn Python for the first time or an experienced hacker looking to expand your skills, Python is an essential language to have in your toolkit.

In the following sections, we will cover the basics of Python programming, including data types, control structures, functions, and classes. We will also explore how Python can be used for web hacking, including web scraping, data analysis, and network programming. By the end of this guide, you will have a solid understanding of Python and how it can be used for hacking purposes.

Python Basics

Before we dive into the world of web hacking, let's start with the basics of Python programming. Python is a versatile language that supports a wide range of data types, control structures, functions, and classes.
Understanding these fundamental concepts will help you write clean, efficient code and make the most of Python's features.

Data Types

Python supports several built-in data types, including

integers, floats, strings, lists, tuples, dictionaries, and sets. These data types allow you to store and manipulate different kinds of information, from simple numbers to complex data structures.

Integers are whole numbers, such as 1, 2, 3, and so on. Floats are numbers with decimal points, such as 3.14 or 2.718. Strings are sequences of characters, enclosed in single or double quotes, such as "hello" or 'world'.

Lists are ordered collections of items, enclosed in square brackets, such as [1, 2, 3]. Tuples are similar to lists but are immutable, meaning their values cannot be changed after they are created. Dictionaries are collections of key-value pairs, enclosed in curly braces, such as {'name': 'Alice', 'age': 30}. Sets are unordered collections of unique items, enclosed in curly braces, such as {1, 2, 3}.

Control Structures

Python supports several control structures, including if statements, for loops, while loops, and try-except blocks.

Chapter 2: Setting Up Your Python Environment

Python is a powerful and versatile programming language that is widely used in various fields, including web development, data analysis, artificial intelligence, and scientific computing. Setting up your Python environment is the first step in getting started with Python programming. In this guide, we will walk you through the process of setting up your Python environment on your computer.

Step 1: Download and Install Python

The first step in setting up your Python environment is to download and install Python on your computer. You can download the latest version of Python from the official Python website (https://www.python.org/). Python is available for Windows, Mac, and Linux operating systems, so make sure to download the appropriate version for your operating system.

Once you have downloaded the Python installer, double-click on it to start the installation process. Follow the on-screen instructions to install Python on your computer. During the installation process, make sure to check the box that says "Add Python to PATH" to ensure that Python is added to your system's PATH environment variable.

After the installation is complete, you can verify that

Python has been installed correctly by opening a command prompt or terminal window and typing "python --version". This command should display the version of Python that you have installed on your computer.

Step 2: Install a Code Editor

While you can write Python code in any text editor, using a dedicated code editor can make your coding experience more efficient and enjoyable. There are several code editors available for Python programming, such as Visual Studio Code, PyCharm, and Sublime Text.

You can download and install a code editor of your choice from the respective websites. Visual Studio Code is a popular choice among Python developers due to its lightweight and customizable nature. PyCharm, on the other hand, is a full-featured integrated development environment (IDE) specifically designed for Python development.

Once you have installed a code editor, you can open it and create a new Python file to start writing your Python code. Most code editors provide features such as syntax highlighting, code completion, and debugging tools to help you write and debug Python code more efficiently.

Step 3: Install Python Packages
Python comes with a standard library that includes a wide range of modules and packages for various tasks. However, you may need to install additional packages to extend the functionality of Python for specific projects. The most popular package manager for Python is pip, which

allows you to easily install and manage Python packages.

To install a Python package using pip, open a command prompt or terminal window and type the following command:
```
```

pip install package_name Replace "package_name" with the name of the package that you want to install. For example, if you want to install the NumPy package for scientific computing, you can use the following command:
```
```

pip install numpy
```
```

You can also install multiple packages at once by separating the package names with spaces:
```
```

pip install package1 package2 package3
```
```

Step 4: Create a Virtual Environment
A virtual environment is a self-contained directory that contains a specific version of Python and its dependencies. Creating a virtual environment for each of your Python projects can help you manage dependencies and avoid conflicts between different projects.

To create a virtual environment, open a command prompt or terminal window and type the following command:
```
```

python -m venv myenv
```
```

Replace "myenv" with the name of your virtual environment. This command will create a new directory with thespecified name that contains a copy of the Python interpreter and the standard library.

To activate the virtual environment, run the following command:
```
```
source myenv/bin/activate
```
```

On Windows, you can activate the virtual environment by running the following command:
``` ``` myenv\Scripts\activate
```
```

Once the virtual environment is activated, any Python packages that you install using pip will be installed in the virtual environment rather than the global Python installation. This allows you to keep your project dependenciesisolated from other projects.

Step 5: Install Jupyter Notebook
Jupyter Notebook is a popular web-based interactive computing environment that allows you to create and share documents that contain live code, equations, visualizations, and narrative text. Jupyter Notebook supports over 40 programming languages, including Python, and is widely used for data analysis, machine learning, and scientific research.

To install Jupyter Notebook, you can use pip to install the jupyter package:
```

```
pip install jupyter
```

After installing Jupyter Notebook, you can start the Jupyter Notebook server by running the following command:

```
jupyter notebook
```

This will open a new tab in your web browser with the Jupyter Notebook interface, where you can create new notebooks, write Python code, and run code cells interactively. Jupyter Notebook also allows you to export notebooks in various formats, such as HTML, PDF, and Markdown.

```
```

Chapter 3: Understanding Basic Python Syntax

Python is a high-level, interpreted programming language known for its simplicity and readability. It is widely used in various fields such as web development, data science, artificial intelligence, and more. Understanding the basic syntax of Python is essential for beginners to start writing code and creating programs effectively. In this article, we will explore the fundamental concepts of Python syntax to help you grasp the language's structure and rules.

Comments: Comments are used to explain the code and make it more readable for other programmers. In Python, comments start with the hash symbol (#) and continue until the end of the line. Comments are ignored by the interpreter and do not affect the program's execution. For example:

```
# This is a comment in Python
```

Variables: Variables are used to store data values in Python. A variable is created by assigning a value to it using the equal sign (=) operator. Variable names can contain letters, numbers, and underscores but cannot start with a number. Python is case-sensitive, so "myVariable" and "myvariable" are considered different variables. For example:

```
x = 10
y = "Hello, World!"
```

Data Types: Python supports various data types such as integers, floats, strings, lists, tuples, dictionaries, and more. The type() function can be used to determine the data type of a variable. For example:

```
x = 10
print(type(x)) # Output:

y = 3.14
print(type(y)) # Output:

z = "Hello, World!" print(type(z)) # Output:
```

Operators: Python supports various operators such as arithmetic, comparison, logical, assignment, and bitwise operators. Arithmetic operators are used to perform mathematical operations, comparison operators are used to compare values, logical operators are used to combine conditions, assignment operators are used to assign values to variables, and bitwise operators are used to perform bitwise operations. For example:

```
x = 10
y = 5

print(x + y) # Output: 15 print(x > y) # Output: True
print(x and y) # Output: 5 x += y
print(x) # Output: 15
```

Control Structures: Control structures such as if-else statements, loops, and functions are used to control the flow of a program. If-else statements are used to make decisions based on conditions, loops are used to repeat a block of code, and functions are used to group code into reusable blocks. For example:

```
x = 10

if x > 5:
print("x is greater than 5")else:
print("x is less than or equal to 5")

for i in range(5):
print(i)
```

```python
def greet(name):
print("Hello, " + name)greet("World")
```

Indentation: Python uses indentation to define blocks of code. Indentation is crucial in Python as it determines the scope of statements. Blocks of code that belong together are indented at the same level. For example:

```python
x = 10

if x > 5:
print("x is greater than 5")
print("This statement is inside the if block")else:
print("x is less than or equal to 5")
print("This statement is inside the else block")
```

Functions: Functions are used to group code into reusable blocks. A function is defined using the def keyword followed by the function name and parameters. The return statement is used to return a value from a function. For example:

```python
def add(x, y):
return x + y

result = add(10, 5) print(result) # Output: 15
```

Lists: Lists are used to store multiple items in a single variable. Lists are mutable, meaning their elements can be changed. Lists are defined using square brackets [] and can contain any data type. For example:

```python
fruits = ["apple", "banana", "cherry"] print(fruits) # Output: ['apple', 'banana', 'cherry']
```

Loops: Loops are used to iterate over a sequence of items. Python supports for loops and while loops. For loops are used to iterate over a sequence of items, while loops are used to repeat a block of code until a condition is met. For example:

```
for i in range(5):
print(i)
```

```
x = 0
while x < 5:
print(x)x += 1
```

Modules: Modules are files containing Python code that can be imported into other Python programs. Modules are used to organize code and make it reusable. Python has a vast standard library with built-in modules that provide various functionalities. For example:

```
import math print(math.sqrt(16)) # Output:
```

Chapter 4: Data Types and Variables in Python

Python is a versatile programming language that is widely used in various fields such as web development, data analysis, artificial intelligence, and more. One of the fundamental concepts in Python programming is data types and variables. Understanding data types and variables is crucial for writing efficient and effective Python code.

In Python, a data type is a classification of data that determines the possible values that can be stored, the operations that can be performed on the data, and the way the data is stored in memory. Python has several built-in data types, such as integers, floats, strings, lists, tuples, dictionaries, and sets. Each data type has its own characteristics and methods that can be used to manipulate the data.

Variables, on the other hand, are used to store data values in memory. A variable is a named storage location that can hold different types of data. Variables are used to store data values that can be manipulated and accessed throughout the program. In Python, variables are created by assigning a value to a name using the assignment operator (=).

Let's take a closer look at some of the common data types and variables in Python:

Integers: Integers are whole numbers without any decimal point. In Python, integers are represented by the int data type. Integers can be positive, negative, or zero. For example, x = 5 is an integer variable with a value of 5.

Floats: Floats are numbers with a decimal point. In Python, floats are represented by the float data type. Floats can be used to represent real numbers with decimal values. For example, y = 3.14 is a float variable with a value of 3.14.

Strings: Strings are sequences of characters enclosed in

single or double quotes. In Python, strings are represented by the str data type. Strings can be used to store text data such as names, addresses, and messages. For example, name = "John" is a string variable with a value of "John".

Lists: Lists are ordered collections of items enclosed in square brackets []. In Python, lists are represented by the list data type. Lists can contain elements of different data types and can be modified using various methods. For example, numbers = [1, 2, 3, 4, 5] is a list variable containing integers.

Tuples: Tuples are ordered collections of items enclosed in parentheses (). In Python, tuples are represented by the tuple data type. Tuples are similar to lists but are immutable, meaning they cannot be modified after creation. For example, coordinates = (3, 4) is a tuple variable containing two integers.

Dictionaries: Dictionaries are unordered collections of key-value pairs enclosed in curly braces {}. In Python, dictionaries are represented by the dict data type. Dictionaries can be used to store data in a key-value format for easy retrieval. For example, person = {"name": "Alice", "age": 30} is a dictionary variable containing a name and age.

Sets: Sets are unordered collections of unique items enclosed in curly braces {}. In Python, sets are represented by the set data type. Sets can be used to perform set operations such as union, intersection, and difference. For example, numbers = {1, 2, 3, 4, 5} is a set variable containing unique integers.

Now that we have covered some of the common data types and variables in Python, let's explore how to work with them in Python code.

Variables in Python are created by assigning a value to a name using the assignment operator (=). For example, x = 5 creates a variable named x with a value of 5. Variables can be reassigned to different values at any time. For example, x = 10 changes the value of x to 10.

Data types in Python are automatically determined based on the value assigned to a variable. For example, x = 5 creates an integer variable, while y = 3.14 creates a float variable. Python is a dynamically typed language, meaning that variables can change data types during runtime. For example, x = 5 assigns an integer value to x, while x = "hello" assigns a string value to x.

Python provides built-in functions to convert between different data types. For example, the int() function can be used to convert a float to an integer, while the float() function can be used to convert an integer to a float. The str() function can be used to convert any data type to a string.

Python also supports type checking using the type() function. The type() function returns the data type of a variable. For example, type(x) returns for an integer variable x, while type(y) returns for a float variable y.

Chapter 5: Control Flow and Loops

Control flow and loops are essential components of any programming language. They allow developers to execute specific code blocks based on certain conditions or repeatedly execute a block of code until a certain condition is met. In this article, we will explore control flow and loops in programming languages and how they can be used to create efficient and powerful programs.

Control Flow:

Control flow refers to the order in which the code is executed in a program. It allows developers to control the flow of execution based on certain conditions or criteria. There are several control flow structures in programming languages, including if-else statements, switch statements, and loops.

If-else statements:

If-else statements are one of the most common control flow structures in programming languages. They allow developers to execute a specific block of code if a certain condition is true, and another block of code if the condition is false. Here's an example of an if-else statement in Python:

```python
python x = 10

if x > 5:
print("x is greater than 5")else:
```

```
print("x is less than or equal to 5")
```

In this example, if the value of x is greater than 5, the program will print "x is greater than 5". Otherwise, it will print "x is less than or equal to 5".

Switch statements:

Switch statements are another control flow structure that allows developers to execute different blocks of code based on the value of a variable. While not all programming languages support switch statements, they are widely used in languages like C, C++, and Java. Here's an example of a switch statement in C++:

```cpp
int x = 2;

switch(x) {case 1:
cout << "x is 1";break;
case 2:
cout << "x is 2";break;

default:
cout << "x is not 1 or 2";
}
```

In this example, if the value of x is 1, the program will print "x is 1". If the value of x is 2, it will print "x is 2".Otherwise, it will print "x is not 1 or 2".

Loops:

Loops are another important control flow structure in programming languages. They allow developers to execute a block of code repeatedly until a certain condition is met. There are several types of loops in programming languages, including for loops, while loops, and do-while loops.

For loops:

For loops are used when the number of iterations is known in advance. They allow developers to iterate over a sequence of values and execute a block of code for each value. Here's an example of a for loop in JavaScript:

```javascript
for (let i = 0; i < 5; i++) {console.log(i);
}
```

In this example, the for loop will iterate from 0 to 4 and print the value of i for each iteration.While loops:
While loops are used when the number of iterations is not known in advance. They allow developers to repeatedly execute a block of code until a certain condition is met. Here's an example of a while loop in Java:

```java
int i = 0;

while (i < 5) { System.out.println(i);  i++;
}
```

In this example, the while loop will continue to execute as long as the value of i is less than 5. It will print the value of i for each iteration.

Do-while loops:

Do-while loops are similar to while loops, but they execute the block of code at least once before checking the

condition. Here's an example of a do-while loop in C#:

```csharp
int i = 0;

do { Console.WriteLine(i); i++;
} while (i < 5);
```

In this example, the do-while loop will execute the block of code at least once, regardless of the condition. It will continue to execute as long as the value of i is less than 5.

Control flow and loops are essential components of any programming language. They allow developers to create efficient and powerful programs by controlling the flow of execution and repeating certain blocks of code. By mastering control flow and loops, developers can write clean, readable, and maintainable code that can handle complex logic and data processing.

Chapter 6: Functions and Modules

Functions and modules are essential concepts in programming languages that allow developers to organize and reuse code effectively. In this article, we will explore the significance of functions and modules in programming languages, their differences, and how they can be used to improve code readability and maintainability.

Functions are blocks of code that perform a specific task or calculation. They take input parameters, perform operations on them, and return a result. Functions can be called multiple times within a program, making them a powerful tool for code reuse and organization. They help break down complex tasks into smaller, more manageable chunks, making code easier to understand and maintain.

Modules, on the other hand, are collections of related functions and variables that can be imported and used in other parts of a program. Modules help organize code by grouping related functionality together, making it easier to manage and maintain large codebases. They also promote code reuse by allowing developers to import and use functions from one module in another module.

One key difference between functions and modules is scope. Functions have local scope, meaning that variables defined within a function are only accessible within that function. On the other hand, modules have global scope, meaning that variables and functions defined within a module can be accessed from any part of a program that imports the module.

Functions and modules work together to create modular and organized code. Functions encapsulate specific tasks or calculations, while modules group related functions and variables together. By using functions within modules, developers can create reusable code that can be easily imported and used in different parts of a program.

Functions and modules are fundamental concepts in programming languages such as Python, JavaScript, and Java. In Python, functions are defined using the def keyword, followed by the function name and parameters. Modules are created by saving a collection of functions and variables in a .py file, which can then be imported and used in other Python scripts.

In JavaScript, functions are defined using the function keyword, followed by the function name and parameters. Modules are created using the export keyword to make functions and variables available for import in other JavaScript files. In Java, functions are defined within classes using the public keyword, while modules are created using packages to organize related classes and functions.

Functions and modules play a crucial role in improving code readability and maintainability. By breaking down complex tasks into smaller functions and organizing related functions and variables into modules, developers can create more modular and organized code. This makes it easier to understand, debug, and modify code, leading to more efficient and reliable software development.

Functions and modules also promote code reuse, allowing developers to import and use functions and variablesfrom one module in another module. This reduces duplication of code and promotes a more efficient and scalable development process. By creating reusable functions and modules, developers can save time and effortby leveraging existing code in new projects.

In conclusion, functions and modules are essential concepts in programming languages that help developers organize and reuse code effectively. Functions encapsulate specific tasks or calculations, while modules group related functions and variables together. By using functions within modules, developers can create modular and organized code that is easier to understand, maintain, and reuse. Functions and modules play a crucial role in improving code readability and maintainability, making them essential tools for software development.

Chapter 7: Working with Strings

Working with strings in any programming language is a fundamental skill that every developer should possess. Strings are used to represent text data, such as names, addresses, and messages, in a program. They are one of the most commonly used data types in programming and are essential for building applications that interact with users.

In this article, we will explore how to work with strings in programming languages, including common operations such as concatenation, splitting, and formatting. We will also discuss best practices for working with strings and some common pitfalls to avoid.

Creating Strings
In most programming languages, strings are created by enclosing text within quotation marks. For example, in Python, you can create a string like this:

name = "John Doe"
In this example, the variable name is assigned the value "John Doe", which is a string. Strings can also be created using single quotes, double quotes, or triple quotes, depending on the language and the requirements of the string.

Concatenating Strings
Concatenation is the process of combining two or more strings into a single string. This is a common operation in programming when you need to build a string from multiple parts. Most programming languages provide a way to concatenate strings using the + operator. For example, in JavaScript:

var firstName = "John";var lastName = "Doe";
var fullName = firstName + " " + lastName;
In this example, the variables firstName and lastName are concatenated to create the fullName string, which contains "John Doe".

Splitting Strings
Splitting is the process of dividing a string into multiple parts based on a delimiter. This is useful when you need to

extract specific information from a string or parse a string into its individual components. Most programming languages provide a way to split strings using a built-in function or method. For example, in Java:

```
String sentence = "Hello, world!"; String[] words = sentence.split(", ");
```

In this example, the split() method is used to divide the sentence string into an array of words, based on the comma and space delimiter. The words array contains ["Hello", "world!"].

Formatting Strings

Formatting is the process of creating a string with placeholders that can be filled in with dynamic values. This is useful when you need to generate strings that contain variable data, such as user input or calculated values. Most programming languages provide a way to format strings using placeholders or string interpolation. For example, in C#:

```
string name = "John"; int age = 30;
string message = string.Format("My name is {0} and I am {1} years old.", name, age);
```

In this example, the string.Format() method is used to create a formatted string with placeholders {0} and {1}, which are filled in with the values of the name and age variables.

Common String Operations

In addition to concatenation, splitting, and formatting, there are many other common operations that can be performed on strings in programming languages. Some of the most common operations include:

Finding the length of a string: This can be done using a built-in function or method that returns the number of characters in a string. For example, in Python: len("Hello") returns 5.

Accessing individual characters: Strings are indexed, meaning you can access individual characters by their position in the string. For example, in JavaScript: var firstChar = "Hello"[0] returns "H".

Changing case: Strings can be converted to uppercase or lowercase using built-in functions or methods. For example, in Java: String name = "John".toLowerCase() returns "john".

Removing whitespace: Leading and trailing whitespace can be removed from a string using a built-in function or method. For example, in C#: string text = " Hello ".Trim() returns "Hello".

Best Practices for Working with Strings
When working with strings in programming languages, there are some best practices that can help improve the efficiency and readability of your code. Some of these best practices include:

Use string interpolation: Instead of concatenating strings using the + operator, use string interpolation or formatting functions to create dynamic strings with placeholders.

Avoid hardcoding strings: Instead of hardcoding strings directly in your code, use constants or configuration files to store and manage strings that may change in the future.

Validate input: When working with user input or external data, always validate and sanitize strings to prevent security vulnerabilities such as SQL injection or cross-site scripting.

Use built-in functions: Most programming languages provide built-in functions or methods for common string operations, so use them instead of reinventing the wheel.

Consider performance: When working with large strings or performing intensive string operations, consider the performance implications and optimize your code accordingly.

Common Pitfalls to Avoid
While working with strings in programming languages, there are some common pitfalls that developers should be aware of to avoid errors and bugs in their code. Some of these common pitfalls include:

Chapter 8: Handling Lists, Tuples, and Dictionaries

In programming languages like Python, handling lists, tuples, and dictionaries is a fundamental skill that every developer must master. These data structures are essential for storing and manipulating collections of data in an efficient and organized manner. In this article, we will explore how to work with lists, tuples, and dictionaries in Python, and discuss their differences and use cases.

Lists in Python are ordered collections of items that can be of any data type. They are mutable, which means that you can modify the elements of a list after it has been created. Lists are created by placing a sequence of items inside square brackets, separated by commas. For example:

```python
my_list = [1, 2, 3, 4, 5]
```

In the above example, `my_list` is a list containing five integers. You can access individual elements of a list by their index, starting from 0. For example, `my_list[0]` would return the first element of the list, which is 1.

You can also modify elements of a list by assigning new values to them. For example, `my_list[2] = 10` would change the third element of the list to 10. Lists also support various operations such as appending, extending, inserting, and removing elements. These operations allow you to manipulate lists in a variety of ways to suit your needs.

Tuples in Python are similar to lists, but they are immutable, which means that once a tuple is created, you cannot change its elements. Tuples are created by placing a sequence of items inside parentheses, separated by commas. For example:

```python
```

```
my_tuple = (1, 2, 3, 4, 5)
```

In the above example, `my_tuple` is a tuple containing five integers. You can access elements of a tuple in the same way as a list, using their index. However, you cannot modify the elements of a tuple once it has been created.

Tuples are often used to represent fixed collections of data that should not be changed, such as coordinates or settings. They are also commonly used for returning multiple values from a function. For example, a function that calculates the area and perimeter of a rectangle could return these values as a tuple.

Dictionaries in Python are unordered collections of key-value pairs. Each key in a dictionary must be unique, and it is used to access the corresponding value. Dictionaries are created by placing a sequence of key-value pairs inside curly braces, separated by commas and with a colon between the key and value. For example:

```python
my_dict = {'name': 'Alice', 'age': 30, 'city': 'New York'}
```

In the above example, `my_dict` is a dictionary with three key-value pairs. You can access the value associated with a key by using square brackets and the key itself. For example, `my_dict['name']` would return 'Alice'.

Dictionaries are often used to store data in a structured way, where each piece of data is associated with a unique identifier. They are commonly used for representing objects in object-oriented programming, where each attribute of an object is stored as a key-value pair in a dictionary.

Now that we have covered the basics of lists, tuples, and dictionaries in Python, let's explore some common operations that you can perform on these data structures.

Working with Lists:
Accessing Elements: You can access individual elements of a list by their index. For example, `my_list[0]` would return the first element of the list.
Modifying Elements: You can modify elements of a list by assigning new values to them. For example, `my_list[2] = 10` would change the third element of the list to 10.
Appending Elements: You can append new elements to the end of a list using the `append()` method. For example, `my_list.append(6)` would add the number 6 to the end of the list.
Extending Lists: You can extend a list by adding the elements of another list to it using the `extend()` method. For example, `my_list.extend([7, 8, 9])` would add the numbers 7, 8, and 9 to the end of the list.
Inserting Elements: You can insert a new element at a specific index in a list using the `insert()` method. For example, `my_list.insert(2, 20)` would insert the number 20 at index 2 in the list.
Removing Elements: You can remove elements from a list by their value using the `remove()` method. For example, `my_list.remove(3)` would remove the number 3 from the list.

```
```

Chapter 9: File Handling in Python

File handling in Python is a crucial aspect of programming that allows developers to read, write, and manipulate files on their computer. In this article, we will explore the various ways in which Python can handle files, including how to open, read, write, and close files.

Opening and Closing Files
The first step in file handling is to open a file using the `open()` function. This function takes two arguments - the name of the file and the mode in which the file should be opened. The mode can be 'r' for reading, 'w' for writing, or 'a' for appending to an existing file. For example, to open a file named 'example.txt' for reading, you would use the following code:

```python
file = open('example.txt', 'r')
```

Once you have finished working with a file, it is important to close it using the `close()` method. This ensures that any resources associated with the file are released and that the file is properly saved. Failure to close a file can lead to memory leaks and other issues, so it is essential to always close files when you are done with them. Here is an example of how to close a file:

```python file.close()
```

```
```

Reading Files

Once a file has been opened for reading, you can use various methods to read its contents. The `read()` method reads the entire contents of a file and returns it as a string. For example:

```python
content = file.read()print(content)
```

You can also read a file line by line using the `readline()` method. This method reads the next line of the file and returns it as a string. For example:

```python
line = file.readline()print(line)
```

Alternatively, you can use the `readlines()` method to read all the lines of a file and return them as a list ofstrings. For example:

```python
lines = file.readlines()

for line in lines:
print(line)
```

Writing to Files

To write to a file, you must first open it in write mode ('w').

If the file does not exist, Python will create it. If the file already exists, its contents will be overwritten. Here is an example of how to write to a file:

```python
file = open('example.txt', 'w') file.write('Hello, world!')
file.close()
```

To append to an existing file, you can open it in append mode ('a'). This will add new content to the end of the file without overwriting existing content. For example:

```python
file = open('example.txt', 'a') file.write('This is a new line.')
file.close()
```

Handling Exceptions
When working with files, it is important to handle exceptions that may occur. For example, if you try to open a file that does not exist, Python will raise a `FileNotFoundError` exception. To handle this exception, you can use a `try` and `except` block. For example:

```python
try:
file = open('nonexistent.txt', 'r') except
FileNotFoundError:
print('File not found.')
```

It is also a good practice to use the `with` statement when working with files. This ensures that the file is properly

41

closed even if an exception occurs. For example:

```python
with open('example.txt', 'r') as file:
content = file.read()print(content)
```

Working with Binary Files
In addition to text files, Python can also handle binary files. To open a file in binary mode, you can use the 'b'flag. For example, to open a binary file named 'example.bin' for reading, you would use the following code:

```python
file = open('example.bin', 'rb')
```

You can read and write binary data using the `read()` and `write()` methods just like with text files. However, it is important to note that binary files are not human-readable, so you may need to use additional tools to view theircontents.

Working with CSV Files
Python also provides built-in support for working with CSV (Comma-Separated Values) files. The `csv` moduleallows you to easily read and write data in CSV format. For example, to read data from a CSV file named 'data.csv', you would use the following code:

```python
import csv
```

with open('data.csv', 'r') as file:

```
reader = csv.reader(file)for row in reader:
print(row)
```

To write data to a CSV file, you would use the `csv.writer` class. For example:

```python
python import csv

data = [
['Name', 'Age', 'City'],
['Alice', 25, 'New York'],
['Bob', 30, 'Los Angeles'],['Charlie
```

Chapter 10: Introduction to Web Technologies

Web technologies have revolutionized the way we interact with the internet and have become an integral part of our daily lives. From simple websites to complex web applications, web technologies have enabled us to connect, communicate, and transact online in ways that were unimaginable just a few decades ago.

In this introduction to web technologies, we will explore the fundamental concepts, tools, and technologies that power the World Wide Web. We will discuss the history of the web, the key components of web technologies, and the role they play in shaping the digital landscape.

History of the Web

The World Wide Web was invented by Sir Tim Berners-Lee in 1989 while working at CERN, the European Organization for Nuclear Research. His vision was to create a system that would allow researchers to easily share and access information over the internet. He developed the first web browser and web server, laying the foundation for what would become the modern web.

The early web was primarily text-based, with simple HTML pages linked together through hyperlinks. Over time, web technologies evolved to include multimedia content, dynamic web pages, and interactive web applications. The introduction of CSS (Cascading Style Sheets) and JavaScript further enhanced the capabilities of the web, allowing developers to create more visually appealing and interactive websites.

Key Components of Web Technologies

Web technologies encompass a wide range of tools and technologies that work together to create and deliver web content. Some of the key components of web technologies include:

HTML (Hypertext Markup Language): HTML is the standard markup language used to create web pages. It defines the structure and content of a web page using tags and attributes. HTML is the backbone of the web and is essential for creating static web pages.

CSS (Cascading Style Sheets): CSS is used to style and format the visual appearance of a web page. It allows developers to control the layout, colors, fonts, and other design elements of a web page. CSS is essential for creating visually appealing and user-friendly websites.

JavaScript: JavaScript is a programming language that adds interactivity and dynamic behavior to web pages.It is commonly used to create animations, validate forms, and interact with web APIs. JavaScript is essential forcreating interactive web applications.

Web Servers: Web servers are software applications that store and deliver web content to users over the internet. They handle requests from web browsers, retrieve web pages from a database or file system, and sendthe content back to the browser. Popular web servers include Apache, Nginx, and Microsoft IIS.

Web Browsers: Web browsers are software applications that allow users to access and view web pages on the internet. They interpret HTML, CSS, and JavaScript code to render web pages and execute web applications. Popular web browsers include Google Chrome, Mozilla Firefox, and Microsoft Edge.

Web Development Tools: Web development tools are software applications that help developers create, test,and debug web applications. They include text editors, code editors, IDEs (Integrated Development Environments), and browser developer tools. Popular web development tools include Visual Studio Code, Sublime Text, and Chrome DevTools.

Role of Web Technologies

Web technologies play a crucial role in shaping the digital landscape and driving innovation on the internet. They enable businesses to create online storefronts, social media platforms to connect people worldwide, and educational institutions to deliver online courses. Some of the key roles of web technologies include:

E-Commerce: Web technologies have transformed the way we shop and conduct business online. E-commerce platforms allow businesses to sell products and services to customers worldwide, enabling them to reach a global audience and increase their revenue. Popular e-commerce platforms include Shopify, WooCommerce, and Magento.

Social Media: Social media platforms use web technologies to connect people, share content, and build online communities. Platforms like Facebook, Twitter, and Instagram allow users to communicate, collaborate, and share experiences with friends and followers around the world.

Online Education: Web technologies have revolutionized education by making learning accessible and affordable to students worldwide. Online learning platforms like Coursera, Udemy, and Khan Academy offer a wide range of courses and resources to help students enhance their skills and knowledge.

Web Applications: Web technologies power a wide range of web applications, from simple calculators to complex enterprise systems. Web applications allow users to perform tasks, interact with data, and access information online. Popular web applications include Google Docs, Trello, and Slack.

Conclusion

In conclusion, web technologies have transformed the way we interact with the internet and have become an essential part of our daily lives. They enable businesses to reach a global audience, social media platforms to connect people worldwide, and educational institutions to deliver online courses. By understanding the history, key components, and role of web technologies, we can appreciate their impact on the digital landscape and the opportunities they offer for innovation and growth.

Chapter 11: HTTP Requests in Python

HTTP (Hypertext Transfer Protocol) is the foundation of data communication on the World Wide Web. It is a protocol that allows web browsers and servers to communicate and exchange information. In this article, we will discuss the basics of HTTP and how to make HTTP requests in Python using the requests library.

HTTP Basics

HTTP is a protocol that defines how messages are formatted and transmitted over the internet. It is based on a client-server architecture, where the client sends a request to the server, and the server responds with the requested information. The communication between the client and server is done through a series of messages, which are known as HTTP requests and responses.

HTTP requests are typically made up of four parts: the request line, headers, an empty line, and an optional message body. The request line contains the method (GET, POST, PUT, DELETE, etc.), the URL of the resource being requested, and the HTTP version being used. The headers contain additional information about the request, such as the user agent, content type, and cookies. The empty line signifies the end of the headers, and the message body contains any data being sent with the request.

HTTP responses, on the other hand, consist of three parts: the status line, headers, and an optional message body. The status line contains the HTTP version, a status code (such as 200 for success or 404 for not found), and a status message. The headers contain additional information about the response, such as the content type and length. The message body contains the requested information, such as HTML content, images, or JSON data.

Making HTTP Requests in Python

Python provides a powerful library called requests for making HTTP requests. This library simplifies the process of sending and receiving HTTP messages, allowing developers to focus on the logic of their applications rather than the intricacies of the HTTP protocol.

To make an HTTP request in Python using the requests library, you first need to install the library using pip:

```
pip install requests
```

Once the requests library is installed, you can import it into your Python script and start making requests. Here is an example of how to make a simple GET request to a website:

```python
import requests

url = 'https://www.example.com'
response = requests.get(url)

print(response.text)
```

In this example, we import the requests library and specify the URL of the website we want to request. We then use the get method of the requests library to send a GET request to the specified URL. The response object contains information about the response, such as the status code, headers, and content. We can access the content of the response using the text attribute and print it to the console.

You can also send other types of requests, such as POST, PUT, DELETE, and more, using the requests library. Here is an example of how to make a POST request with data:

```python
import requests
```

```
url = 'https://www.example.com'data = {'key': 'value'}
response = requests.post(url, data=data)

print(response.text)
```

In this example, we specify the URL of the website and a dictionary of data that we want to send with the POST request. We use the post method of the requests library to send a POST request with the specified data. We can access the content of the response in the same way as before.

The requests library also provides additional features, such as authentication, cookies, sessions, and more, to make working with HTTP requests even easier. You can find more information about the requests library and its features in the official documentation.

Conclusion

HTTP is a fundamental protocol for communication on the internet, and understanding how it works is essential for web developers. Python provides a powerful library called requests for making HTTP requests, which simplifies the process of sending and receiving data over the web. By using the requests library, developers can focus on building their applications rather than worrying about the intricacies of the HTTP protocol. Whether you are building a web scraper, REST API, or web application, the requests library in Python is a valuable tool for working with HTTP requests.

Chapter 12: Web Scraping Fundamentals

Web scraping is a process of extracting information from websites using automated tools or scripts. It is a powerful technique that allows users to gather data from the internet for various purposes such as research, analysis, and monitoring. In this article, we will discuss the fundamentals of web scraping, including its benefits, techniques, and best practices.

Benefits of Web Scraping:

Web scraping offers several benefits for businesses, researchers, and individuals. Some of the key advantages of web scraping include:

Data Collection: Web scraping allows users to collect large amounts of data from websites quickly and efficiently. This data can be used for various purposes such as market research, competitor analysis, and lead generation.

Automation: Web scraping automates the process of data extraction, saving time and effort for users. Instead of manually copying and pasting information from websites, users can use web scraping tools to extract data in a matter of minutes.

Real-time Data: Web scraping enables users to access real-time data from websites, which can be valuable for monitoring changes in market trends, news updates, and social media activity.

Competitive Advantage: By using web scraping to gather data on competitors, businesses can gain valuableinsights into their strategies, pricing, and product offerings. This information can be used to make informed decisions and stay ahead of the competition.

Customization: Web scraping allows users to customize the data extraction process to suit their specific needs. Users can define the parameters for data extraction, such as keywords, categories, and date ranges, to ensure they get the most relevant information.

Techniques of Web Scraping:

There are several techniques that can be used for web scraping, depending on the complexity of the data and the structure of the website. Some of the common web scraping techniques include:

HTML Parsing: HTML parsing is the process of extracting data from the HTML code of a website. This technique involves analyzing the structure of the HTML code to identify the elements that contain the desiredinformation, such as text, images, and links.

API Integration: Some websites provide APIs (Application Programming Interfaces) that allow users to accesstheir data in a structured format. By integrating with these APIs, users can extract data from websites more easily and efficiently.

Screen Scraping: Screen scraping involves extracting data

from the visual elements of a website, such as text, images, and tables. This technique is useful for extracting data from websites that do not have a well-defined structure or API.

Web Crawling: Web crawling is a technique used to systematically browse the web and extract data from multiple websites. This technique is commonly used by search engines to index web pages and provide relevant search results to users.

Best Practices for Web Scraping:

When performing web scraping, it is important to follow best practices to ensure the process is ethical, legal, and effective. Some of the best practices for web scraping include:

Respect Robots.txt: Robots.txt is a file that websites use to communicate their crawling guidelines to web scrapers. It is important to respect the rules specified in the Robots.txt file to avoid overloading the website's servers and causing disruptions.

Use Proper User Agents: User agents are identifiers that web browsers use to communicate with websites. When performing web scraping, it is important to use a proper user agent that accurately identifies the scraping tool and its purpose.

Limit Requests: To avoid being blocked by websites, it is important to limit the number of requests made during web scraping. Users should space out their requests and use caching techniques to reduce the load on the website's servers.

Monitor Changes: Websites frequently update their content and structure, which can affect the effectiveness of web scraping. It is important to monitor changes in websites and adjust the scraping process accordingly to ensure accurate and up-to-date data.

Data Privacy: When extracting data from websites, it is important to respect the privacy of users and comply with data protection regulations. Users should only extract data that is publicly available and avoid collecting sensitive information without permission.

In conclusion, web scraping is a valuable technique for extracting data from websites for various purposes. By understanding the fundamentals of web scraping, including its benefits, techniques, and best practices, users can effectively gather and analyze data from the internet. Whether you are a business looking to gain a competitive advantage, a researcher conducting market analysis, or an individual seeking real-time information, web scraping can provide valuable insights and opportunities for growth.

Chapter 13: Parsing HTML with Beautiful Soup

Beautiful Soup is a Python library that is commonly used for parsing HTML and XML documents. It provides a simple and intuitive way to navigate and search through the contents of a web page. In this article, we will explore how to use Beautiful Soup to parse HTML documents and extract useful information from them.

To get started with Beautiful Soup, you will need to install the library using pip. You can do this by running the following command in your terminal:

```
pip install beautifulsoup4
```

Once you have installed Beautiful Soup, you can start using it in your Python code. The first step is to import the library:

```python
from bs4 import BeautifulSoup
```

Next, you will need to create a Beautiful Soup object by passing in the HTML content that you want to parse. You can do this by using the `BeautifulSoup` constructor and passing in the HTML content as a string. For example, if you have a simple HTML document like this:

````html

Example Page


Hello, World!

This is an example paragraph.
```

You can parse it using Beautiful Soup like this:

```python html_content="""
Example Page



Hello, World!

This is an example paragraph."""
soup = BeautifulSoup(html_content, 'html.parser')
```

Now that you have created a Beautiful Soup object, you

can start navigating and searching through the HTML content. Beautiful Soup provides several methods for accessing different parts of the document, such as finding elements by tag name, class name, or ID. Here are some examples of how you can use these methods:

```python
# Find the title of the pagetitle = soup.title print(title.text)

# Find the first h1 element on the pageh1 = soup.find('h1')
print(h1.text)

# Find all paragraph elements on the page paragraphs =
soup.find_all('p')
for p in paragraphs:
print(p.text)
```

In addition to finding elements by tag name, class name, or ID, you can also search for elements based on their attributes. For example, if you want to find all `a` elements with a specific class attribute, you can do so like this:

```python
# Find all links with a specific class attribute links =
soup.find_all('a', class_='link')
for link in links:
print(link['href'])
```

You can also navigate through the document by accessing the parent, sibling, and child elements of a particular element. For example, if you want to find the parent element of a specific element, you can do so like this:

```python
# Find the parent element of the first paragraphparent =
soup.find('p').parent print(parent.name)
```

Beautiful Soup also provides a way to extract the text content of an element without any HTML tags. You can do this by using the `get_text()` method on an element. For example, if you want to extract all the text content from a paragraph element, you can do so like this:

```python
# Extract the text content from a paragraph element
paragraph_text        =        soup.find('p').get_text()
print(paragraph_text)
```

In addition to extracting text content, you can also extract attributes from elements using the `get()` method. For example, if you want to extract the `href` attribute from a link element, you can do so like this:

```python
# Extract the href attribute from a link elementlink_href
= soup.find('a')['href'] print(link_href)
```

Beautiful Soup also provides a way to search for elements using regular expressions. This can be useful if you want to find elements based on a specific pattern in their attributes or text content. For example, if you want to find all elements with a specific class attribute that contains the word "link", you can do so like this:

```python
import re

# Find all elements with a class attribute that contains the word "link"
links = soup.find_all(class_=re.compile('link'))
for link in links:
    print(link['href'])
```

In addition to parsing HTML documents, Beautiful Soup can also be used to parse XML documents. The process is very similar to parsing HTML documents, as both types of documents are structured in a similar way. You can use the same methods and techniques to navigate and search through XML documents using Beautiful Soup.

In conclusion, Beautiful Soup is a powerful and versatile library for parsing HTML and XML documents in Python. It provides a simple and intuitive way to navigate and search through the contents of a web page

# Chapter 14: Extracting Data from Websites

In today's digital age, the internet is a treasure trove of information. With millions of websites covering a wide range of topics, extracting data from websites has become an essential skill for businesses, researchers, and individuals looking to gather valuable insights. Whether you are looking to analyze market trends, track competitor activity, or collect research data, web scraping is a powerful tool that can help you extract data from websites efficiently and effectively.

Web scraping, also known as web harvesting or web data extraction, is the process of automatically collecting information from websites. This can include text, images, links, and other types of content that are publicly available on the internet. By using web scraping tools and techniques, you can quickly gather large amounts of data from multiple sources and save valuable time and resources.

There are several methods for extracting data from websites, ranging from manual copying and pasting to using specialized software and programming languages. One of the most popular tools for web scraping is Python, a versatile programming language that is widely used for data analysis and web development. Python offers a variety of libraries and frameworks that make it easy to scrape websites and extract data in a structured format.

One of the key libraries for web scraping in Python is

BeautifulSoup, which allows you to parse HTML and XML documents and extract data using a simple and intuitive syntax. Another popular library is Scrapy, a powerful web crawling and scraping framework that provides a more advanced set of features for extracting data from websites at scale. By combining these tools with other Python libraries such as Requests and Pandas, you can create robust web scraping scripts that can handle complex data extraction tasks with ease.

When extracting data from websites, it is important to be mindful of legal and ethical considerations. While most websites allow web scraping for personal use, some sites may have terms of service that prohibit automated data collection. It is important to review the website's robots.txt file and terms of service before scraping data to ensure compliance with their policies. Additionally, it is recommended to use web scraping tools responsibly and avoid overloading servers with excessive requests, as this can lead to IP blocking or other restrictions.

In addition to Python, there are other tools and techniques that can be used for extracting data from websites. For example, web scraping software such as Octoparse, ParseHub, and WebHarvy provide user-friendly interfaces for creating web scraping agents without the need for programming knowledge. These tools allow you to visually select elements on a webpage and extract data in a point-and-click manner, making it easy to collect data from websites without writing code.

Another approach to web scraping is using browser extensions such as Data Miner, Web Scraper, and Scraper, which allow you to extract data directly from your web browser without the need for external software. These extensions provide a convenient way to scrape data from websites in real-time and export it in various formats such as CSV, Excel, or JSON. By using browser extensions, you can quickly gather data from websites without the need for complex programming or setup.

In addition to tools and techniques, there are also best practices that can help you optimize your web scraping efforts and ensure successful data extraction. Some key tips for extracting data from websites include:

Identify the data you want to extract: Before starting a web scraping project, it is important to define the specific data fields you want to collect from websites. This can include product prices, customer reviews, contact information, or any other relevant information that will help you achieve your goals.

Understand the website structure: Each website is structured differently, with its own layout, design, and coding. Before scraping data from a website, it is important to understand its structure and how data is organized on the page. This will help you identify the elements you need to extract and create an effective scraping strategy.

Use CSS selectors and XPath: When extracting data from websites, CSS selectors and XPath are powerful tools that can help you locate and extract specific elements on a webpage. By using these techniques, you can target specific HTML elements such as links, images, and text and extract them with precision.

Handle pagination and dynamic content: Some websites use pagination or dynamic content loading to display large amounts of data. When scraping these types of websites, it is important to handle pagination and dynamic content properly to ensure that all data is captured. This may involve simulating user interactions, scrolling through pages, or using AJAX requests to load additional content.

Monitor website changes: Websites are constantly evolving, with updates, redesigns, and changes in content. To ensure that your web scraping scripts continue to work effectively, it is important to monitor website changes and adjust your scraping strategy accordingly. This may involve updating CSS selectors, XPath expressions, or other elements of your scraping script to adapt to changes in the website structure.

Overall, extracting data from websites is a valuable skill that can provide valuable insights and information for a wide range of applications.

# Chapter 15: Automating Tasks with Selenium

Automating tasks with Selenium is a powerful tool that can save time and increase efficiency in various tasks. Selenium is an open-source tool that is widely used for automating web browsers. It provides a set of tools and libraries that allow users to interact with web elements, simulate user actions, and perform various tasks on web pages.

One of the main advantages of using Selenium for automation is that it supports multiple programming languages including Java, Python, C#, and Ruby. This makes it a versatile tool that can be used by developers with different programming backgrounds. In this article, we will focus on automating tasks with Selenium in Python.

To get started with automating tasks with Selenium in Python, you will need to install the Selenium library. You can do this by using the pip package manager, which is the standard package manager for Python. To install Selenium, simply run the following command in your terminal:

```
pip install selenium
```

Once you have installed the Selenium library, you can start writing your automation scripts. The first step in automating tasks with Selenium is to create a new instance of the WebDriver class. This class represents the web browser that will be used for automation. You can choose from different web browsers such as Chrome, Firefox, or Safari. In this example, we will use Chrome as the web browser:

```python
from selenium import webdriver

# Create a new instance of the Chrome web browserdriver
= webdriver.Chrome()
```

Next, you can use the WebDriver instance to navigate to a specific URL. This can be done by using the `get` method of the WebDriver class:

```python
# Navigate to a specific URL
driver.get('https://www.example.com')
```

Once you have navigated to a web page, you can interact with the web elements on the page. This can be done by using various methods provided by the WebDriver class such as `find_element_by_id`, `find_element_by_name`, `find_element_by_xpath`, and `find_element_by_css_selector`. These methods allow you to locate specific elements on the web page based on their attributes such as ID, name, XPath, or CSS selector.

For example, if you want to locate an input field on the web page with the ID `username`, you can use the `find_element_by_id` method:

```python
# Locate the input field with the ID 'username'
username_field = driver.find_element_by_id('username')
```

Once you have located the web element, you can interact with it by sending keys, clicking on it, or performing other actions. For example, if you want to enter a username into the input field, you can use the `send_keys` method:

```python
# Enter a username into the input field
username_field.send_keys('john_doe')
```

Similarly, you can locate other web elements on the page and interact with them using the methods provided by the WebDriver class. This allows you to automate various tasks such as filling out forms, clicking on buttons, and navigating through different pages on a website.

In addition to interacting with web elements, Selenium also provides methods for performing other tasks such as taking screenshots, handling alerts and pop-ups, and executing JavaScript code on the web page. These methods allow you to perform a wide range of tasks while automating web browsers with Selenium.

For example, if you want to take a screenshot of the current web page, you can use the `save_screenshot` method:

```python
# Take a screenshot of the current web page
driver.save_screenshot('screenshot.png')
```

Similarly, if you want to handle an alert that appears on the web page, you can use the `switch_to.alert` method:

```python
# Switch to the alert and accept it alert =
driver.switch_to.alert alert.accept()
```

Overall, automating tasks with Selenium in Python is a powerful tool that can save time and increase efficiency in various tasks. By using the Selenium library and the WebDriver class, you can interact with web elements, simulate user actions, and perform a wide range of tasks on web pages. Whether you are automating testing processes, web scraping, or any other task that involves interacting with web browsers, Selenium is a versatile tool that can help you achieve your goals.

In conclusion, automating tasks with Selenium in Python is a valuable skill that can benefit developers, testers, and anyone who works with web browsers on a regular basis. By using the Selenium library and the WebDriver class, you can automate various tasks on web pages, saving time and increasing efficiency. Whether you are automating testing processes, web scraping, or any other task that involves interacting with web elements on a web page, Selenium provides the tools and libraries you need to get the job done.

# Chapter 16: Interacting with APIs
# Interacting with APIs in Python

Application Programming Interfaces (APIs) are an essential part of modern software development. They allow different software systems to communicate with each other, enabling developers to access and use the functionalities of other services or applications. In this article, we will explore how to interact with APIs in Python, one of the most popular programming languages for web development.

What is an API?

An API is a set of rules and protocols that allow different software systems to communicate with each other. It defines the methods and data formats that applications can use to request and exchange information. APIs are commonly used to access the functionalities of web services, such as social media platforms, payment gateways, and cloud storage services.

There are different types of APIs, including RESTful APIs, SOAP APIs, and GraphQL APIs. RESTful APIs are the most common type of API and are widely used in web development. They use HTTP methods, such as GET, POST, PUT, and DELETE, to perform CRUD (Create, Read, Update, Delete) operations on resources.

Interacting with APIs in Python

Python is a versatile and powerful programming language that is widely used in web development, data science, and machine learning. It has a rich set of libraries and tools that make it easy to interact with APIs and consume web services. In this section, we will explore how to interact with APIs in Python using the requests library.

The requests library is a popular HTTP library for Python that allows you to send HTTP requests and receive HTTP responses from web servers. It provides a simple and intuitive interface for making API calls and handling the response data. To install the requests library, you can use the following command:

```python
pip install requests
```

Once you have installed the requests library, you can start making API calls in Python. Here is an example of how to make a GET request to a RESTful API endpoint using the requests library:

```python
import requests

url = 'https://api.example.com/users' response = requests.get(url)

if response.status_code == 200: data = response.json()
print(data)
else:
```

```
print('Error:', response.status_code)
```

In this example, we import the requests library and define the URL of the API endpoint that we want to access. We then make a GET request to the API endpoint using the `requests.get()` function, which returns a response object. We check the status code of the response to ensure that the request was successful (status code 200), and then parse the JSON data from the response using the `response.json()` method.

Handling API Authentication

Many APIs require authentication to access their functionalities. There are different authentication methods that APIs use, such as API keys, OAuth tokens, and basic authentication. In this section, we will explore how to authenticate with APIs in Python using the requests library.

API keys are a common authentication method used by many APIs. An API key is a unique identifier that is used to authenticate API requests and track usage. To authenticate with an API using an API key, you can include the key in the request headers or as a query parameter. Here is an example of how to authenticate with an API using an API key in Python:

```python
import requests

url = 'https://api.example.com/users' api_key =
```

```
'your_api_key'
headers = {'Authorization': f'Bearer {api_key}'}response =
requests.get(url, headers=headers)
if response.status_code == 200:
data = response.json()print(data)
else:
print('Error:', response.status_code)
```

In this example, we define the API key as a variable and
include it in the request headers using the
`Authorization` header. This tells the API server that we
are authorized to access the API functionalities. We then
make a GET request to the API endpoint with the
authenticated headers.

Handling Pagination

Many APIs return paginated responses to limit the number
of results returned in a single request. Pagination is a
common practice used by APIs to improve performance
and reduce the load on the server. To retrieve all the
results from a paginated API endpoint, you need to make
multiple requests and concatenate the results.

In this section, we will explore how to handle pagination in
Python when interacting with APIs. Here is an example of
how to retrieve all the results from a paginated API
endpoint using the requests library:

```python
import requests
```

```
url = 'https://api.example.com/users'params = {'page': 1}
results = []

while True:
response = requests.get(url, params=params)

if response.status_code == 200: data = response.json()
results.extend(data['results'])

if 'next' in data['links']:
url = data['links']['next']else:
breakelse:
print('Error:', response.status_code)break

print(results
)
```
```

# Chapter 17: Networking for Hackers

Networking is a crucial aspect of the modern world, connecting people, devices, and systems across vast distances. For hackers, understanding networking is essential for carrying out various tasks, from gathering information to launching attacks. In this guide, we will explore the fundamentals of networking for hackers, including key concepts, protocols, and tools.

What is Networking?

Networking refers to the practice of connecting multiple devices and systems to share resources and information.
```

This can be done through various means, such as wired or wireless connections. In the context of hacking, networking plays a vital role in communicating with target systems, gathering data, and carrying out attacks.

Key Concepts in Networking

To understand networking for hackers, it is essential to grasp some key concepts. These include:

IP Addresses: An IP address is a unique identifier assigned to each device on a network. It allows devices to communicate with each other over the internet or local network. IP addresses can be either IPv4 or IPv6, with the former being more common.

Subnetting: Subnetting is the practice of dividing a large network into smaller subnetworks. This helps in optimizing network performance and security by segmenting traffic and resources.

Ports: Ports are virtual endpoints for communication in a network. Each port is associated with a specific protocol or service, such as HTTP (port 80) or FTP (port 21). Understanding ports is crucial for hackers to identify vulnerabilities and exploit them.

Protocols: Protocols are rules and standards that govern communication between devices on a network. Common protocols include TCP/IP, UDP, HTTP, and FTP. Hackers need to be familiar with these protocols to manipulate network traffic effectively.

Networking Protocols

Networking protocols are essential for establishing communication between devices on a network. Some common protocols used in networking include:

TCP/IP: Transmission Control Protocol/Internet Protocol (TCP/IP) is the foundation of the internet and most networks. It provides reliable, connection-oriented communication between devices.

UDP: User Datagram Protocol (UDP) is a connectionless protocol that allows for faster communication but with less reliability than TCP. It is commonly used for streaming media and online gaming.

HTTP: Hypertext Transfer Protocol (HTTP) is used for transferring web pages and other data over the internet. It is the foundation of the World Wide Web.

FTP: File Transfer Protocol (FTP) is used for transferring files between devices on a network. It is commonly used for uploading and downloading files from servers.

Networking Tools for Hackers

Hackers rely on a variety of tools to carry out their activities on networks. Some common networking tools used by hackers include:

Nmap: Nmap is a powerful network scanning tool that allows hackers to discover devices on a network, identify open ports, and gather information about services running on those ports.

Wireshark: Wireshark is a network protocol analyzer that captures and analyzes network traffic in real-time. It allows hackers to inspect packets, identify vulnerabilities, and troubleshoot network issues.

Metasploit: Metasploit is a popular penetration testing framework that helps hackers identify and exploit vulnerabilities in network systems. It provides a wide range of exploits and payloads for carrying out attacks.

Netcat: Netcat is a versatile networking tool that can be used for various purposes, such as port scanning, file transfer, and remote shell access. It is often referred to as the "Swiss Army knife" of networking tools.

Conclusion

Networking is a fundamental aspect of hacking, enabling hackers to communicate with target systems, gather information, and carry out attacks. By understanding key networking concepts, protocols, and tools, hackers can navigate networks effectively and exploit vulnerabilities to achieve their goals. This guide provides a basic introduction to networking for hackers, laying the groundwork for further exploration and learning in this dynamic field.

# Chapter 18: Socket Programming in Python

Socket programming in Python is a powerful tool that allows programmers to create networked applications. By using sockets, developers can establish communication between different devices over a network, enabling data exchange and remote control of devices. In this article, we will explore the basics of socket programming in Python, including how to create and use sockets, establish connections, and send and receive data.

What is a Socket?

A socket is a communication endpoint that allows two devices to communicate with each other over a network. In socket programming, a socket is identified by a unique address called an IP address and a port number. The IP address identifies the device on the network, while the port number identifies the specific application or service running on the device.

There are two types of sockets in socket programming: client sockets and server sockets. Client sockets are used to initiate a connection with a server socket, while server sockets are used to listen for incoming connections from client sockets.

Creating a Socket

In Python, the socket module provides the necessary functions and classes to create and use sockets. To create a socket, you first need to import the socket module:

```
import socket
```

Next, you can create a socket object using the socket()
function:

```
s = socket.socket(socket.AF_INET,
socket.SOCK_STREAM)
```

The socket() function takes two arguments: the address
family (AF_INET for IPv4) and the socket type
(SOCK_STREAM for TCP sockets). In this example, we
are creating a TCP socket for IPv4 communication.

Establishing a Connection

To establish a connection with a server socket, you need to
know the IP address and port number of the server.Once
you have this information, you can use the connect()
method of the socket object to connect to the server:

```
s.connect(("127.0.0.1", 8080))
```

In this example, we are connecting to a server running on
the local machine (127.0.0.1) on port 8080. If the
connection is successful, the connect() method returns
without raising an exception.

Sending and Receiving Data

Once a connection is established, you can send and receive
data over the socket. To send data, you can use thesend()

method of the socket object:

```
s.send(b"Hello, World!")
```

The send() method takes a bytes object as an argument. In this example, we are sending the string "Hello, World!" encoded as bytes using the b prefix.

To receive data, you can use the recv() method of the socket object:

```
data = s.recv(1024)
```

The recv() method takes the maximum number of bytes to receive as an argument. In this example, we arereceiving up to 1024 bytes of data from the server.

Closing the Connection

After sending and receiving data, it is important to close the connection to release network resources. You can use the close() method of the socket object to close the connection:

```
s.close()
```

The close() method closes the socket connection and frees up any resources associated with the socket. Example: Simple Client-Server Application
To demonstrate socket programming in Python, let's create a simple client-server application. In this example, the server will listen for incoming connections from client

sockets and echo back any data received.

Server Code:

```
import socket
```

```
server           =           socket.socket(socket.AF_INET,
socket.SOCK_STREAM)server.bind(("127.0.0.1", 8080))
server.listen(1)
```

```
print("Server listening on port 8080")
```

```
client, address = server.accept() print(f"Connection from
{address}")
```

```
data       =       client.recv(1024)       print(f"Received:
{data.decode()}")
```

```
client.send(data)
```

```
client.close()server.close()
```

Client Code:

```
import socket
```

```
client           =           socket.socket(socket.AF_INET,
socket.SOCK_STREAM)        client.connect(("127.0.0.1",
8080))
client.send(b"Hello, Server!") data = client.recv(1024)
print(f"Received: {data.decode()}")
```

```
client.close()
```

In this example, the server creates a socket, binds it to the local address and port, and listens for incoming connections. When a client connects, the server accepts the connection, receives data from the client, and sends it back to the client. The client creates a socket, connects to the server, sends data to the server, and receives the echoed data.

Conclusion

Socket programming in Python is a powerful tool for creating networked applications. By using sockets, developers can establish communication between different devices over a network, enabling data exchange and remote control of devices. In this article, we explored the basics of socket programming in Python, including how to create and use sockets, establish connections, and send and receive data. With this knowledge, you can start building your own networked applications using Python.

# Chapter 19: Exploiting Network Protocols

Network protocols are a set of rules and conventions that govern the way data is transmitted over a network. They define how devices communicate with each other, how data is formatted and structured, and how errors are handled. Network protocols are essential for ensuring that information is transmitted accurately and efficiently across a network.

However, network protocols can also be exploited by malicious actors to gain unauthorized access to a network, steal sensitive information, or disrupt network operations. By understanding how network protocols work and identifying their vulnerabilities, attackers can exploit these weaknesses to carry out cyber attacks.

In this article, we will explore the various ways in which network protocols can be exploited by attackers and discuss some of the measures that can be taken to protect against these threats.

Common Network Protocol Exploits

There are several common techniques that attackers use to exploit network protocols. These include:

Man-in-the-middle attacks: In a man-in-the-middle attack, an attacker intercepts communication between two parties and can eavesdrop on the conversation, modify messages, or impersonate one of the parties. This type of attack is often carried out by exploiting vulnerabilities in protocols such as HTTP, FTP, or SMTP.

Denial of Service (DoS) attacks: DoS attacks overwhelm a network or server with a flood of traffic, causing it to become slow or unresponsive. Attackers can exploit vulnerabilities in protocols such as TCP/IP or UDP to launch DoS attacks and disrupt network operations.

Packet sniffing: Packet sniffing involves capturing and analyzing network traffic to steal sensitive information such as passwords, credit card numbers, or other confidential data. Attackers can exploit vulnerabilities in protocols such as Ethernet, IP, or TCP to intercept packets and extract valuable information.

Spoofing attacks: Spoofing attacks involve impersonating a legitimate user or device to gain unauthorized access to a network. Attackers can exploit vulnerabilities in protocols such as ARP or DNS to spoof IP addresses, MAC addresses, or domain names and deceive network devices into accepting malicious traffic.

Protocol fuzzing: Protocol fuzzing is a technique used to discover vulnerabilities in network protocols by sending malformed or unexpected data to a target system. Attackers can exploit these vulnerabilities to crash a network service, execute arbitrary code, or gain unauthorized access to a network.

Protecting Against Network Protocol Exploits

To protect against network protocol exploits, organizations

can implement a variety of security measures. These include:

Encrypting network traffic: Encrypting network traffic using protocols such as SSL/TLS can help protect sensitive information from being intercepted by attackers. By encrypting data in transit, organizations can ensure that it remains confidential and secure.

Implementing access controls: Implementing access controls such as firewalls, intrusion detection systems, and authentication mechanisms can help prevent unauthorized access to a network. By restricting access to network resources based on user credentials or device characteristics, organizations can reduce the risk of exploitation.

Keeping software up to date: Keeping network devices, operating systems, and applications up to date with the latest security patches can help protect against known vulnerabilities. By regularly updating software, organizations can address security flaws and reduce the risk of exploitation.

Monitoring network traffic: Monitoring network traffic for suspicious activity or anomalies can help detect and respond to potential attacks. By analyzing network logs, traffic patterns, and behavior, organizations can identify signs of exploitation and take corrective action to mitigate the threat.

Conducting security assessments: Regularly conducting

security assessments such as penetration testing or vulnerability scanning can help identify weaknesses in network protocols and address them before they are exploited by attackers. By proactively testing network security controls, organizations can improve their overall security posture and reduce the risk of exploitation.

Conclusion

Network protocols are essential for enabling communication and data exchange across a network. However, they can also be exploited by attackers to carry out cyber attacks and gain unauthorized access to sensitive information. By understanding the vulnerabilities in network protocols and implementing security measures to protect against exploitation, organizations can reduce the risk of network breaches and safeguard their data and resources.

It is important for organizations to stay informed about emerging threats and best practices for securing network protocols. By staying vigilant and proactive in addressing security risks, organizations can effectively defend against network protocol exploits and maintain the integrity and confidentiality of their network infrastructure.

# Chapter 20: Packet Manipulation with Scapy

Packet manipulation is a crucial aspect of network security and analysis. It involves modifying the content of data packets as they travel across a network, allowing for various actions such as filtering, monitoring, and even attacking. One powerful tool for packet manipulation is Scapy, a Python library that enables users to create, send, sniff, and manipulate packets at a low level.

Scapy is a versatile and flexible tool that can be used for a wide range of tasks, from network reconnaissance and analysis to penetration testing and network troubleshooting. In this article, we will explore the basics of packet manipulation with Scapy, including how to create and send packets, sniff network traffic, and manipulate packetcontent.

Creating and Sending Packets

One of the primary functions of Scapy is to create and send custom packets across a network. This can be useful for testing network infrastructure, identifying vulnerabilities, or conducting penetration testing. To create a new packet in Scapy, you can use the `IP()` function to define the IP header and the `TCP()` function to define the TCP header. For example, the following code snippet creates a simple TCP packet:

```python
from scapy.all import *
```

```
packet = IP(dst="192.168.1.1")/TCP(dport=80)
```

In this example, we create a new packet with an IP destination address of "192.168.1.1" and a TCP destination port of 80. To send the packet, we can use the `send()` function:

```python
send(packet)
```

This will send the packet across the network to the specified destination address and port. Scapy also provides additional functions for sending packets, such as `sr1()` for sending a packet and receiving a response, and `sr()` for sending multiple packets and receiving responses.

Sniffing Network Traffic

Another important feature of Scapy is its ability to sniff network traffic in real-time. This can be useful for monitoring network activity, analyzing network protocols, and identifying potential security threats. To sniff network traffic with Scapy, you can use the `sniff()` function. For example, the following code snippet sniffs network traffic and prints the packet details:

```python
from scapy.all import *

def packet_handler(packet):
```

```
print(packet.show())

sniff(prn=packet_handler)
```

In this example, we define a `packet_handler()` function
that prints the details of each packet that is sniffed. We
then call the `sniff()` function with the
`packet_handler()` function as an argument, which will
capture and print each packet that is detected on the
network.

Manipulating Packet Content

One of the most powerful features of Scapy is its ability to
manipulate the content of packets. This can be useful for
modifying packet headers, payload data, and other packet
attributes. For example, the following code snippet
modifies the source IP address of a packet:

```python
from scapy.all import *

packet = IP(dst="192.168.1.1")/TCP(dport=80) packet.src
= "10.0.0.1"

send(packet)
```

In this example, we create a new packet with an IP
destination address of "192.168.1.1" and a TCP destination

port of 80. We then modify the source IP address of the packet to "10.0.0.1" before sending it across the network. This demonstrates how easy it is to manipulate packet content with Scapy.

Conclusion

Packet manipulation with Scapy is a powerful tool for network security professionals, penetration testers, and network administrators. By creating, sending, sniffing, and manipulating packets at a low level, users can gain valuable insights into network activity, identify vulnerabilities, and test network infrastructure. Scapy's flexibility and versatility make it an essential tool for anyone working in the field of network security and analysis. With its intuitive Python interface and extensive documentation, Scapy is an excellent choice for packet manipulation tasks of all kinds.

# Chapter 21: Introduction to Black Hat Techniques

lack hat techniques refer to unethical and manipulative strategies used by individuals or organizations to achieve their goals online. These techniques are often used to deceive search engines, manipulate rankings, and gain an unfair advantage over competitors. While black hat techniques may provide short-term gains, they can have serious consequences in the long run, including penalties from search engines, loss of credibility, and damage to a brand's reputation.

In this article, we will explore the various black hat techniques used in the digital marketing world, their impact on businesses, and how to avoid falling victim to these unethical practices.

Keyword stuffing is one of the most common black hat techniques used by marketers to manipulate search engine rankings. This practice involves overloading web pages with keywords in an attempt to trick search engines into ranking the page higher in search results. While keywords are an important part of SEO, keywordstuffing can make content unreadable and harm the user experience. Search engines like Google have strict guidelines against keyword stuffing and penalize websites that engage in this practice.

Another black hat technique is cloaking, where a website shows different content to search engines and users. This deceptive practice involves presenting one version of a web page to search engine crawlers to improve rankings, while showing a different version to users. Cloaking is a violation of search engine guidelines and can result in penalties or even removal from search engine results pages.

Link farming is another black hat technique used to manipulate search engine rankings. This practice involves creating a network of websites that link to each other in an attempt to artificially inflate the number of backlinks pointing to a website. While backlinks are an important ranking factor, quality is more important than quantity. Search engines like Google have algorithms in place to detect link farms and penalize websites that engage in this practice.

Duplicate content is another black hat technique that involves copying content from other websites and publishing it on your own site. Duplicate content can harm your website's rankings and credibility, as search engines may have difficulty determining which version of the content is original. It is important to create unique, high-quality content that provides value to users and sets your website apart from competitors.

Black hat techniques can also include negative SEO tactics, such as building spammy backlinks to a competitor's website in an attempt to harm their rankings. These unethical practices can have serious consequences for businesses, including loss of organic traffic, lower search engine rankings, and damage to brand reputation.

To avoid falling victim to black hat techniques, businesses should focus on ethical and sustainable SEO practices. This includes creating high-quality, original content that provides value to users, optimizing website performance and user experience, and building a strong, natural backlink profile. By following search engine guidelines and focusing on delivering a positive user experience, businesses can improve their online visibility and build a strong, reputable brand.

In conclusion, black hat techniques are unethical practices used to manipulate search engine rankings and gain an unfair advantage online. While these techniques may provide short-term gains, they can have serious consequences in the long run. By focusing on ethical SEO practices and providing value to users, businesses can improve their online visibility and build a strong, reputable brand. It is important to stay informed about the latest SEO trends and guidelines to avoid falling victim to black hat techniques and protect your online presence.

# Chapter 22: Reconnaissance and Information Gathering

Reconnaissance and information gathering are critical components of any successful operation, whether it be military, corporate, or even personal. These processes involve gathering intelligence on a target to assess its strengths, weaknesses, and vulnerabilities. By understanding the terrain, the enemy's capabilities, and their intentions, one can better plan and execute a successful mission.

In the military context, reconnaissance is the act of gathering information about an enemy or potential enemy. This can involve various methods, including aerial surveillance, ground patrols, and cyber reconnaissance. By collecting data on the enemy's troop movements, equipment, and defenses, military commanders can make informed decisions about how to engage the enemy effectively.

Information gathering, on the other hand, involves collecting data on a target's infrastructure, personnel, and operations. This can include conducting interviews, analyzing public records, and monitoring social media activity. By understanding the target's organizational structure, communication channels, and vulnerabilities, one can identify potential points of entry and exploit them to achieve the desired outcome.

In the corporate world, reconnaissance and information gathering are essential for competitive intelligence. By gathering data on competitors, market trends, and customer preferences, companies can make informed decisions about product development, marketing strategies, and business expansion. This can involve monitoring industry publications, attending trade shows, and conducting market research to gather valuable insights that can give a company a competitive edge.

In the realm of cybersecurity, reconnaissance and information gathering are critical for identifying potential threats and vulnerabilities in a network. Hackers often use reconnaissance techniques such as port scanning, social engineering, and phishing attacks to gather information about a target's systems and exploit weaknesses. By conducting regular security audits, monitoring network traffic, and implementing robust security measures, organizations can protect their data and infrastructure from malicious actors.

Overall, reconnaissance and information gathering are essential components of any successful operation, whether it be military, corporate, or cybersecurity. By collecting and analyzing data on a target, one can better understand their strengths and weaknesses and develop a strategic plan to achieve their objectives.

There are several key principles to keep in mind when

conducting reconnaissance and information gathering:

Define your objectives: Before embarking on any reconnaissance mission, it is essential to clearly define your goals and objectives. What information are you trying to gather? What are the potential risks and rewards of obtaining this information? By setting clear objectives, you can focus your efforts and resources on achieving your desired outcome.

Conduct thorough research: Research is a critical component of reconnaissance and information gathering. This can involve analyzing open-source intelligence, conducting interviews, and monitoring online activity. By gathering as much information as possible, you can build a comprehensive picture of your target and identify potential vulnerabilities.

Use a variety of methods: Reconnaissance and information gathering require a diverse range of methods and techniques. This can include physical surveillance, social engineering, and technical reconnaissance. By using a combination of methods, you can gather a more complete picture of your target and increase your chances of success.

Maintain operational security: Operational security, or OPSEC, is essential when conducting reconnaissance and information gathering. This involves protecting sensitive information, maintaining a low profile, and minimizing the risk of detection. By following OPSEC protocols, you can reduce the likelihood of compromising your mission and achieving your objectives.

Continuously assess and adapt: Reconnaissance and information gathering are dynamic processes that require constant assessment and adaptation. As the situation evolves, it is essential to reassess your objectives, methods, and tactics to ensure you are on track to achieve your goals. By remaining flexible and responsive, you can overcome obstacles and achieve success.

In conclusion, reconnaissance and information gathering are essential components of any successful operation, whether it be military, corporate, or cybersecurity. By gathering intelligence on a target, one can better understand their strengths and weaknesses and develop a strategic plan to achieve their objectives. By following key principles such as defining objectives, conducting thorough research, using a variety of methods, maintaining operational security, and continuously assessing and adapting, one can increase their chances of success and achieve their desired outcome.

## Chapter 23: Fundamentals of Exploiting Vulnerabilities in Systems

Exploiting vulnerabilities in systems is a critical aspect of cybersecurity that involves identifying weaknesses in a system's defenses and using them to gain unauthorized access or cause harm. In this article, we will explore the fundamentals of exploiting vulnerabilities in systems, including common types of vulnerabilities, methods of exploitation, and best practices for protecting against exploitation.

Vulnerabilities can exist in various components of a system, including software, hardware, and network configurations. Common types of vulnerabilities include buffer overflows, SQL injection, cross-site scripting, and insecure authentication mechanisms. These vulnerabilities can be exploited by attackers to gain access to sensitive information, disrupt system operations, or compromise the integrity of the system.

One of the most common methods of exploiting vulnerabilities is through the use of malware, which is malicious software designed to exploit weaknesses in a system's defenses. Malware can be delivered through various means, including email attachments, infected websites, and removable media. Once installed on a system, malware can perform a variety of malicious actions, such as stealing sensitive data, encrypting files for ransom, or launching denial-of-service attacks.

Another common method of exploiting vulnerabilities is through the use of social engineering, which involves manipulating individuals into divulging sensitive information or performing actions that compromise the security of a system. Social engineering techniques can include phishing emails, phone calls pretending to be from a trusted source, or impersonating a legitimate user to gain access to restricted areas of a system.

In addition to malware and social engineering, attackers can also exploit vulnerabilities through the use of exploit kits, which are prepackaged tools that automate the process of identifying and exploiting vulnerabilities in systems. Exploit kits are often used in conjunction with other attack techniques to maximize the chances of success and minimize the effort required by the attacker.

To protect against exploitation, organizations must implement a comprehensive cybersecurity strategy that includes regular vulnerability assessments, patch management, and user awareness training. Vulnerability assessments involve scanning systems for known vulnerabilities and prioritizing them based on their severity and potential impact. Patch management involves applying security updates and patches to systems in a timely manner to address known vulnerabilities and minimize the risk of exploitation.

User awareness training is also critical for protecting against exploitation, as many vulnerabilities are the result of human error or negligence. By educating users about the risks of social engineering, phishing attacks, and other common attack techniques, organizations can help prevent unauthorized access and data breaches.

In conclusion, exploiting vulnerabilities in systems is a fundamental aspect of cybersecurity that requires a thorough understanding of common vulnerabilities, methods of exploitation, and best practices for protection. By implementing a comprehensive cybersecurity strategy that includes vulnerability assessments, patch management, and user awareness training, organizations can minimize the risk of exploitation and protect their systems from unauthorized access and data breaches.

# Chapter 24: SQL Injection Attacks

SQL injection attacks are a type of security vulnerability that occurs when an attacker is able to manipulate the input of a web application in order to gain unauthorized access to a database. This type of attack can have serious consequences, as it allows the attacker to view, modify, or delete sensitive data from the database. In thisarticle, we will discuss what SQL injection attacks are, how they work, and how to prevent them.

What is SQL Injection?

SQL injection is a type of attack that targets the SQL (Structured Query Language) database management system. It occurs when an attacker is able to manipulate the input of a web application in order to executemalicious SQL queries. These queries can be used to retrieve, modify, or delete data from the database, potentially exposing sensitive information such as usernames, passwords, and credit card numbers.

SQL injection attacks can occur in any web application that uses SQL to interact with a database. This includes websites, online stores, and web-based applications. Attackers typically exploit vulnerabilities in the application's input validation process, allowing them to inject malicious SQL code into the database query.

How Does SQL Injection Work?

SQL injection attacks work by exploiting vulnerabilities in the way that a web application handles user input. When a user submits a form on a website, the application typically processes the input and constructs an SQL query to retrieve the requested data from the database. If the input is not properly sanitized or validated, an attacker can manipulate it to inject malicious SQL code.

For example, consider a simple login form on a website that uses the following SQL query to authenticate users: SELECT * FROM users WHERE username = 'input_username' AND password = 'input_password'
If the application does not properly sanitize the input fields, an attacker could input the following username and password:

Username: ' OR '1'='1 Password: ' OR '1'='1

The resulting SQL query would look like this:

SELECT * FROM users WHERE username = '' OR '1'='1' AND password = '' OR '1'='1'

Since '1'='1' is always true, the query would return all records from the users table, effectively bypassing the authentication process and allowing the attacker to log in as any user.

Types of SQL Injection Attacks

There are several types of SQL injection attacks that attackers can use to exploit vulnerabilities in a web application. The most common types include:

In-band SQL Injection: This is the most common type of SQL injection attack, where the attacker is able to retrieve data from the database using the same communication channel as the attack. In-band attacks can be further divided into two subtypes:

Error-based SQL Injection: In this type of attack, the attacker is able to retrieve data from the database by causing an error in the SQL query. The error message returned by the database can contain sensitive information, such as table names or column names.

Union-based SQL Injection: In this type of attack, the attacker is able to retrieve data from the database by using the UNION operator to combine the results of two separate queries into a single result set.

Blind SQL Injection: In blind SQL injection attacks, the attacker is not able to retrieve data from the database directly. Instead, the attacker uses Boolean-based or time-based techniques to infer information about the database by analyzing the application's response to different inputs.

Out-of-band SQL Injection: In out-of-band attacks, the attacker is able to retrieve data from the database using a separate communication channel, such as DNS or HTTP requests. This type of attack is less common but can be effective in certain scenarios.

Preventing SQL Injection Attacks

Preventing SQL injection attacks requires a combination of secure coding practices, input validation, and parameterized queries. Here are some best practices to help protect your web application from SQL injection attacks:

Use Parameterized Queries: Parameterized queries are SQL statements that use placeholders for input values, which are then bound to parameters at runtime. This prevents attackers from injecting malicious SQL code into the query.

Sanitize Input: Always sanitize user input by validating and escaping special characters before using it in an SQL query. This can help prevent attackers from injecting malicious code into the database.

Use Stored Procedures: Stored procedures are precompiled SQL statements that can be called from the application. By using stored procedures, you can reduce the risk of SQL injection attacks by limiting the input that can be passed to the database.

Limit Database Permissions: Restrict the permissions of the database user used by the web application to only the necessary privileges. This can help prevent attackers from accessing sensitive data or modifying the database schema.

Implement Web Application Firewalls: Web application firewalls can help protect your web application from SQL injection attacks by monitoring and filtering incoming traffic for malicious SQL queries.

Regularly Update Software: Keep your web application and database software up to date with the latest security patches.

# Chapter 25: Cross-Site Scripting (XSS) Attacks Cross-Site Scripting (XSS) Attacks

Cross-Site Scripting (XSS) is a type of security vulnerability commonly found in web applications. It allows an attacker to inject malicious scripts into web pages viewed by other users. XSS attacks can be used to steal sensitive information, such as login credentials, session tokens, or personal data, from unsuspecting users. In this article, we will explore the different types of XSS attacks, how they work, and how to prevent them.

Types of XSS Attacks

There are three main types of XSS attacks: reflected XSS, stored XSS, and DOM-based XSS.

Reflected XSS: Reflected XSS attacks occur when a user input is reflected back to the user without proper sanitization. An attacker can craft a malicious URL that contains a script, which is then executed by the victim's browser when they visit the URL. This type of attack is typically used in phishing scams, where the attacker tricks the victim into clicking on a malicious link.

Stored XSS: Stored XSS attacks occur when a user input is stored on the server and displayed to other users without proper sanitization. This type of attack is more dangerous than reflected XSS because the malicious script is permanently stored on the server and can affect multiple users. Attackers can use stored XSS to steal sensitive information from a large number of users or to deface a website.

DOM-based XSS: DOM-based XSS attacks occur when a web application uses client-side scripts to manipulate the Document Object Model (DOM) of a web page. An attacker can exploit vulnerabilities in the client-side scripts to inject malicious code into the DOM, which is then executed by the victim's browser. Thistype of attack is more difficult to detect and prevent than traditional XSS attacks.

How XSS Attacks Work

XSS attacks work by exploiting vulnerabilities in web applications that allow user input to be executed as code. Attackers can use various techniques to inject malicious scripts into web pages, such as:

Inserting tags into form fields, URL parameters, or cookies.
Using JavaScript events, such as onclick or onmouseover, to trigger the execution of malicious code.
Encoding special characters, such as , and ", to bypass input validation and inject scripts.
Using social engineering techniques to trick users into executing malicious scripts, such as by disguising them as legitimate links or buttons.

Once the malicious script is injected into a web page, it can perform various actions, such as:

Stealing cookies or session tokens to hijack user sessions.

Logging keystrokes to capture sensitive information, such as passwords.
Redirecting users to phishing websites to steal their credentials.
Defacing websites by modifying the content of web pages.
Preventing XSS Attacks

To prevent XSS attacks, web developers should follow best practices for secure coding and implement various security measures, such as:

Input validation: Validate and sanitize all user input to prevent malicious scripts from being executed. Use input validation libraries, such as OWASP ESAPI, to filter out dangerous characters and encode special characters.

Output encoding: Encode all output data before displaying it to users to prevent XSS attacks. Use output encoding libraries, such as OWASP AntiSamy, to sanitize HTML, CSS, and JavaScript code.

Content Security Policy (CSP): Implement a Content Security Policy to restrict the sources of executable scripts, stylesheets, and other resources on a web page. CSP can help prevent XSS attacks by blocking malicious scripts from being loaded from unauthorized domains.

HTTP headers: Set secure HTTP headers, such as X-XSS-Protection and X-Content-Type-Options, to protect against XSS attacks. These headers can help prevent browsers from executing malicious scripts and enforcing strict content type policies.

Secure cookies: Use secure and HttpOnly flags for cookies to prevent them from being accessed by malicious scripts. Secure cookies should only be transmitted over HTTPS connections and should not be accessible to client-side scripts.

Regular security audits: Conduct regular security audits and penetration testing to identify and patch vulnerabilities in web applications. Use automated tools, such as OWASP ZAP and Burp Suite, to scan for XSS vulnerabilities and other security issues.

Conclusion

Cross-Site Scripting (XSS) attacks are a common and dangerous threat to web applications. By understanding how XSS attacks work and implementing best practices for secure coding, web developers can protect their applications from malicious scripts and prevent sensitive information from being stolen. It is important to stay informed about the latest security threats and vulnerabilities and to regularly update and patch web applications to prevent XSS attacks. By following the recommendations outlined in this article, developers can help ensure the security and integrity of their web applications.

# Chapter 26: Remote Code Execution (RCE)

Remote Code Execution (RCE) is a type of security vulnerability that allows an attacker to execute arbitrary code on a target system remotely. This type of vulnerability is considered one of the most severe security issues as it can lead to complete compromise of the target system, allowing attackers to take full control of the system and access sensitive data.

RCE vulnerabilities can exist in various types of software, including web applications, mobile applications, and network services. Attackers can exploit these vulnerabilities by sending specially crafted input to the target system, which allows them to execute malicious code on the system.

There are several ways in which RCE vulnerabilities can be exploited by attackers. One common method is through injection attacks, where attackers inject malicious code into input fields or parameters of a web application. This code is then executed by the application, leading to RCE on the target system.

Another method of exploiting RCE vulnerabilities is through deserialization attacks. Deserialization is the process of converting data into a format that can be stored or transmitted. Attackers can exploit deserialization vulnerabilities to execute arbitrary code on the target system by manipulating the serialized data sent to the application.

RCE vulnerabilities can have severe consequences for organizations and individuals. Attackers can use RCE to steal sensitive data, disrupt services, or launch further attacks on other systems. Therefore, it is crucial for organizations to identify and patch RCE vulnerabilities in their software to protect against potential attacks.

There are several ways to prevent RCE vulnerabilities in software. One of the most effective methods is to sanitize input data to ensure that it does not contain any malicious code. Organizations should also regularly update their software to patch known vulnerabilities and implement security measures such as firewalls and intrusion detection systems to detect and prevent RCE attacks.

In conclusion, Remote Code Execution (RCE) is a severe security vulnerability that allows attackers to execute arbitrary code on a target system remotely. Organizations and individuals should take steps to identify and patch RCE vulnerabilities in their software to protect against potential attacks and safeguard sensitive data. By implementing security best practices and staying vigilant against emerging threats, organizations can reduce the risk of falling victim to RCE attacks and ensure the security of their systems.

# Chapter 27: Exploiting Authentication and Authorization

Authentication and authorization are two crucial components of any secure system. Authentication is the process of verifying the identity of a user, while authorization is the process of determining what actions a user is allowed to perform within a system. In this article, we will explore how attackers can exploit authentication and authorization vulnerabilities to gain unauthorized access to sensitive information and resources.

One common way attackers exploit authentication vulnerabilities is through password guessing attacks. Password guessing attacks involve repeatedly trying different passwords until the correct one is found. This can be done manually by an attacker or automated using tools such as password cracking software. Weak passwords, such as "123456" or "password," are particularly vulnerable to password guessing attacks.

To protect against password guessing attacks, organizations should enforce strong password policies that require users to create complex passwords that are difficult to guess. Additionally, organizations should implement account lockout mechanisms that temporarily lock an account after a certain number of failed login attempts. This can help prevent attackers from gaining unauthorized access even if they are able to guess a user's password.

Another common way attackers exploit authentication vulnerabilities is through phishing attacks. Phishing attacks involve tricking users into revealing their login credentials by posing as a legitimate entity, such as a bank or social media website. Attackers may send phishing emails that contain links to fake login pages that look identical to the legitimate website. When users enter their login credentials on these fake pages, the attackers capture the information and use it to gain unauthorized access to the user's account.

To protect against phishing attacks, organizations should educate users about the dangers of phishing and how to recognize phishing emails. Users should be encouraged to verify the legitimacy of emails and websites before entering any sensitive information. Additionally, organizations can implement multi-factor authentication (MFA) mechanisms that require users to provide an additional form of verification, such as a one-time code sent to their mobile device, in addition to their password.

In addition to exploiting authentication vulnerabilities, attackers may also exploit authorization vulnerabilities to gain unauthorized access to sensitive information and resources. Authorization vulnerabilities occur when a system fails to properly enforce access controls, allowing users to perform actions that they should not be allowed to perform.

One common way attackers exploit authorization vulnerabilities is through privilege escalation attacks. Privilege escalation attacks involve gaining higher levels of access within a system than the attacker is entitled to. For example, an attacker may exploit a vulnerability in a web application to gain administrative privileges, allowing them to access and modify sensitive information.

To protect against privilege escalation attacks, organizations should implement strong access control mechanismsthat restrict users' access to only the resources and actions that are necessary for their role. Organizations should also regularly review and update access control policies to ensure that users have the appropriate level of access.

Another way attackers exploit authorization vulnerabilities is through insecure direct object references (IDOR). IDOR vulnerabilities occur when a system exposes internal object references, such as database keys or file paths,in its user interface. Attackers can manipulate these references to access unauthorized resources or perform unauthorized actions.

To protect against IDOR vulnerabilities, organizations should implement proper input validation and output encoding to prevent attackers from manipulating object references. Additionally, organizations should use indirect object references, such as unique identifiers that are mapped to internal object references, to preventattackers from directly accessing sensitive resources.

In conclusion, authentication and authorization are critical components of any secure system. By understanding how attackers exploit authentication and authorization vulnerabilities, organizations can take proactive steps to protect against unauthorized access to sensitive information and resources. Implementing strong password policies, educating users about phishing attacks, enforcing access controls, and mitigating privilege escalation and IDOR vulnerabilities are essential steps in securing authentication and authorization mechanisms. By taking these measures, organizations can reduce the risk of unauthorized access and protect their systems from malicious attackers.

# Chapter 28: Bypassing Security Mechanisms

Bypassing security mechanisms in programming languages is a common practice among hackers and malicious actors seeking to exploit vulnerabilities in software systems. This can lead to data breaches, financial losses, and other serious consequences for individuals and organizations. In this article, we will explore some common techniques used to bypass security mechanisms in programming languages and how developers can protect their systems from such attacks.

One of the most common ways to bypass security mechanisms in programming languages is through code injection. Code injection involves inserting malicious code into a program to exploit vulnerabilities and gain unauthorized access to a system. This can be done through various means, such as SQL injection, cross-site scripting, and buffer overflow attacks.

SQL injection is a type of code injection that targets databases by inserting malicious SQL statements into input fields on a website. This can allow attackers to manipulate databases, steal sensitive information, or even take control of the entire system. To prevent SQL injection attacks, developers should use parameterized queries and input validation to sanitize user input and prevent malicious code from being executed.

Cross-site scripting (XSS) is another common technique used to bypass security mechanisms in programming languages. XSS attacks involve injecting malicious scripts into web pages to steal cookies, session tokens, or other sensitive information from users. To prevent XSS attacks, developers should use input validation and output encoding to sanitize user input and prevent malicious scripts from being executed in the browser.

Buffer overflow attacks are a type of code injection that targets memory buffers in a program to overwrite data and execute arbitrary code. This can lead to system crashes, privilege escalation, and other serious security vulnerabilities. To prevent buffer overflow attacks, developers should use secure coding practices, such as bounds checking and input validation, to prevent buffer overflows and other memory-related vulnerabilities.

In addition to code injection, attackers can also bypass security mechanisms in programming languages through other means, such as reverse engineering, social engineering, and cryptographic attacks. Reverse engineering involves decompiling and analyzing software to discover vulnerabilities and exploit them for malicious purposes. Social engineering involves manipulating individuals to disclose sensitive information or perform unauthorized actions. Cryptographic attacks involve breaking encryption algorithms to decrypt sensitive data or forge digital signatures.

To protect against these types of attacks, developers should use secure coding practices, such as input validation, output encoding, and secure communication protocols, to prevent vulnerabilities in their software systems. They should also regularly update their software and libraries to patch known security vulnerabilities and stay informed about the latest security threats and best practices.

In conclusion, bypassing security mechanisms in programming languages is a serious threat that can lead to data breaches, financial losses, and other serious consequences for individuals and organizations. By using secure coding practices and staying informed about the latest security threats, developers can protect their systems from malicious attacks and ensure the integrity and confidentiality of their data. It is essential for developers to be proactive in addressing security vulnerabilities and implementing robust security measures to safeguard their software systems from potential threats.

# Chapter 29: Cryptography for Hackers

Cryptography is a vital tool in the world of hacking. It is the practice and study of techniques for secure communication in the presence of third parties. It involves creating and analyzing protocols that prevent third parties or the public from reading private messages. Cryptography is used in various aspects of hacking, including securing communication, data encryption, and authentication.

One of the main uses of cryptography in hacking is to secure communication between hackers. When hackers communicate with each other, they want to ensure that their messages are not intercepted by third parties.
Cryptography allows hackers to encrypt their messages so that only the intended recipients can read them. This helps to prevent eavesdropping and ensures that sensitive information remains confidential.

Data encryption is another important use of cryptography in hacking. When hackers store sensitive information on their devices or servers, they want to ensure that this data is secure and cannot be accessed by unauthorized users. Cryptography allows hackers to encrypt their data so that even if it is stolen or hacked, it cannot be read without the decryption key. This helps to protect sensitive information and prevent data breaches.

Authentication is also a key aspect of cryptography in hacking. When hackers access systems or networks, they need to prove their identity to gain access. Cryptography allows hackers to use digital signatures and certificates to authenticate themselves and prove that they are who they claim to be. This helps to prevent unauthorized access and ensures that only legitimate users can access sensitive information.

There are various types of cryptographic algorithms and protocols that hackers can use to secure their communication, encrypt their data, and authenticate themselves. Some of the most common cryptographic algorithms include RSA, AES, and SHA. These algorithms use mathematical techniques to encrypt and decrypt data, ensuring that it remains secure and confidential.

RSA (Rivest-Shamir-Adleman) is a widely used public-key cryptosystem that is used for secure communication and data encryption. It uses two keys, a public key and a private key, to encrypt and decrypt data. The public key is used to encrypt data, while the private key is used to decrypt it. This ensures that only the intended recipient can read the encrypted data.

AES (Advanced Encryption Standard) is a symmetric-key encryption algorithm that is used for securing data. It uses a single key to encrypt and decrypt data, making it faster and more efficient than public-key encryption.
AES is widely used in various applications, including secure communication, data encryption, and file encryption.

SHA (Secure Hash Algorithm) is a cryptographic hash function that is used to generate a fixed-size hash value from input data. This hash value is unique to the input data and can be used to verify the integrity of the data. SHA is commonly used in digital signatures, certificates, and password hashing.

In addition to these cryptographic algorithms, hackers can also use cryptographic protocols to secure their communication and data. Some of the most common cryptographic protocols include SSL/TLS, PGP, and IPsec.

SSL (Secure Sockets Layer) and its successor, TLS (Transport Layer Security), are cryptographic protocols that are used to secure communication over the Internet. They use encryption and authentication to ensure that data transmitted between clients and servers remains secure and confidential. SSL/TLS is commonly used in web browsers, email clients, and other applications to protect sensitive information.

PGP (Pretty Good Privacy) is a cryptographic protocol that is used for secure email communication. It uses public-key encryption to encrypt and decrypt email messages, ensuring that only the intended recipient can read them. PGP is widely used by hackers and other users to protect their email communication from eavesdropping and interception.

IPsec (Internet Protocol Security) is a suite of protocols that is used to secure communication over IP networks. It provides encryption, authentication, and integrity protection for data transmitted between devices. IPsec is commonly used in VPNs (Virtual Private Networks) to secure remote access and private communication.

Overall, cryptography is a vital tool for hackers in securing their communication, encrypting their data, and authenticating themselves. By using cryptographic algorithms and protocols, hackers can protect their sensitive information from unauthorized access and ensure that their communication remains confidential. Cryptography plays a crucial role in the world of hacking and is essential for maintaining security and privacy in the digital age.

# Chapter 30: Password Cracking Techniques

Password cracking is a process used by hackers to gain unauthorized access to a system or account by guessing or decrypting the password. There are various techniques and tools that hackers use to crack passwords, and it is important for individuals and organizations to be aware of these techniques in order to protect themselves from potential security threats.

One of the most common password cracking techniques is known as brute force attack. This method involves trying every possible combination of characters until the correct password is found. While this technique can be effective, it is also time-consuming and resource-intensive. Hackers may use specialized software or tools to automate the process and speed up the cracking process.

Another common password cracking technique is known as dictionary attack. This method involves using a pre-defined list of commonly used passwords or words to try and guess the password. Hackers may use password dictionaries that contain thousands or even millions of commonly used passwords, as well as variations of these passwords (such as adding numbers or special characters). This technique is often more effective than brute force attack, as it targets the most likely passwords first.

Rainbow table attack is another popular password cracking technique that hackers use. This method involves pre- computing a large number of hashes for possible passwords and storing them in a table. When a hacker obtains the hash of a password, they can then look up the corresponding plaintext password in the rainbow table to quickly crack the password. This technique is particularly effective for cracking passwords that are stored using weak hashing algorithms.

Social engineering is another technique that hackers use to crack passwords. This method involves manipulating individuals into revealing their passwords through deception or manipulation. For example, a hacker may impersonate a trusted individual or organization and trick the victim into providing their password. Social engineering attacks can be difficult to detect and prevent, as they often rely on human psychology rather than technical vulnerabilities.

Phishing is a common form of social engineering attack that hackers use to steal passwords. This method involves sending fraudulent emails or messages to individuals, asking them to provide their login credentials or personal information. The emails may appear to be from a legitimate source, such as a bank or online service, in order to trick the victim into revealing their password. Phishing attacks can be highly effective, especially if the victim is not aware of the signs of a fraudulent email.

Keylogging is another technique that hackers use to crack passwords. This method involves installing malicious software on a victim's device to record their keystrokes and capture their login credentials. Keyloggers can be difficult to detect, as they operate silently in the background without the user's knowledge. Hackers can then use the captured passwords to gain unauthorized access to the victim's accounts.

In addition to these techniques, hackers may also use password spraying, credential stuffing, and other advancedmethods to crack passwords. Password spraying involves trying a small number of commonly used passwords against multiple accounts, while credential stuffing involves using stolen login credentials from one website to gain access to other websites. These techniques can be highly effective, especially if individuals reuse passwordsacross multiple accounts.

To protect against password cracking attacks, individuals and organizations should follow best practices forpassword security. This includes using strong, unique passwords for each account, enabling multi-factor authentication whenever possible, and regularly updating passwords to prevent unauthorized access.
Additionally, individuals should be cautious of phishing emails and messages, and avoid clicking on links or providing personal information to unknown sources.

Overall, password cracking is a serious security threat that individuals and organizations should be aware of. By understanding the various techniques and tools that hackers use to crack passwords, individuals can take steps toprotect themselves and their sensitive information from potential security breaches. It is important to stay vigilant and proactive in order to safeguard against password cracking attacks and maintain the security of personal and sensitive data.

# Chapter 31: Steganography and Data Hiding

Steganography and data hiding are two techniques used to conceal information within other forms of data, such as images, audio files, or text. These techniques are often used to protect sensitive information from unauthorized access or to communicate covertly. In this article, we will explore the concepts of steganography and data hiding, their applications, and how they can be implemented in different languages.

Steganography is the practice of concealing a message, image, or file within another file in such a way that the existence of the hidden data is not obvious. The word steganography is derived from the Greek words "steganos," meaning covered or concealed, and "graphy," meaning writing. Steganography has been used for centuries as a means of secret communication, with examples dating back to ancient Greece and Rome.

Data hiding, on the other hand, is a broader term that encompasses various techniques for concealing data within other data. While steganography is a specific form of data hiding that focuses on hiding data within media files, data hiding techniques can also be applied to text files, databases, and other forms of digital data.

There are several reasons why someone might want to use steganography or data hiding techniques. One common use case is to protect sensitive information from being intercepted or accessed by unauthorized parties. By concealing data within other files, individuals can communicate securely without drawing attention to the factthat they are exchanging sensitive information.

Another use case for steganography and data hiding is digital watermarking, which involves embedding information within media files to verify their authenticity or ownership. For example, photographers may embed hidden watermarks in their images to prevent unauthorized use or reproduction of their work.

Steganography and data hiding can also be used for covert communication, espionage, and other clandestine activities. For example, spies and intelligence agencies may use steganography to exchange secret messages without alerting potential adversaries to the existence of the communication.

Implementing steganography and data hiding techniques in different programming languages requires a good understanding of the underlying principles and algorithms. One common approach to steganography is to embeddata within the least significant bits of a digital file, such as an image or audio file. By modifying these bits, it is possible to conceal information without significantly altering the appearance or quality of the file.

In Python, one popular library for steganography is Stegano, which provides a simple interface for hiding and extracting data from images. To hide a message in an image using Stegano, you can use the following code snippet:

```
from stegano import lsb

# Hide a message in an image
lsb.hide("original_image.png",              "secret_message",
"output_image.png")
```

This code snippet hides the message "secret_message" within the image "original_image.png" and saves the resulting image as "output_image.png." To extract the hidden message from the image, you can use the following

code snippet:

```
from stegano import lsb

# Extract a message from an image message =
lsb.reveal("output_image.png") print(message)
```

This code snippet extracts the hidden message from the image "output_image.png" and prints it to the console. The Stegano library makes it easy to implement steganography in Python and experiment with different techniques for hiding and extracting data from images.

In Java, steganography can be implemented using the JSteg library, which provides a set of classes and methods for hiding and extracting data from images. To hide a message in an image using JSteg, you can use the following code snippet:

```
```

import com.jhlabs.image.ChannelMixFilter;

// Hide a message in an image
ChannelMixFilter filter = new ChannelMixFilter();
filter.hideMessage("original_image.png", "secret_message", "output_image.png");
```
```

This code snippet uses the ChannelMixFilter class from the JSteg library to hide the message "secret_message" within the image "original_image.png" and save the resulting image as "output_image.png." To extract the hidden message from the image, you can use the following code snippet:

```
```

import com.jhlabs.image.ChannelMixFilter;

// Extract a message from an image ChannelMixFilter
filter = new ChannelMixFilter();
String message = filter.revealMessage("output_image.png");
System.out.println(message);
```
```

This code snippet extracts the hidden message from the image "output_image.png" and prints it to the console. The JSteg library provides a powerful set of tools for implementing steganography in Java and experimenting

122

with different techniques for hiding and extracting data from images.

In C++, steganography can be implemented using the OpenStego library, which provides a set of classes and functions for hiding and extracting data from images. To hide a message in an image using OpenStego, you can use the following code snippet:

``` #include

# Chapter 32: Reverse Engineering

Reverse engineering is the process of analyzing a product or system to understand how it works, without the aid of its original design or documentation. This practice is commonly used in various fields, such as software development, mechanical engineering, and electronics, to gain insights into the design and functionality of a product or system.

In the context of software development, reverse engineering involves decompiling a compiled program to understand its source code and algorithms. This can be useful for understanding how a particular software application works, identifying potential security vulnerabilities, or creating interoperable software components.

Reverse engineering can also be used in mechanical engineering to analyze the design and construction of a
```

physical product. By disassembling and examining the components of a product, engineers can gain a better understanding of its functionality and improve upon its design.

In the field of electronics, reverse engineering is used to understand the internal workings of electronic devices, such as circuit boards and microchips. This can be helpful for troubleshooting issues, identifying counterfeit components, or creating compatible replacements.

The process of reverse engineering typically involves several steps, including:

Acquisition of the product or system: The first step in reverse engineering is obtaining the product or system to be analyzed. This can involve purchasing a commercial product, acquiring a sample from a competitor, or obtaining a copy of the software or hardware to be analyzed.

Disassembly: The next step is to disassemble the product or system to access its internal components. This may involve removing screws, opening casings, or using specialized tools to access the internal components.

Analysis: Once the product or system has been disassembled, the next step is to analyze its components and functionality. This may involve studying the design of the product, examining the materials used, and identifying key components.

Reverse engineering tools: In many cases, specialized

tools and software are used to aid in the reverse engineering process. These tools may include decompilers, disassemblers, and other software tools that can help analyze the product or system.

Documentation: Finally, the results of the reverse engineering process are typically documented in a report or other format. This documentation may include diagrams, schematics, and other information that can be used to understand the design and functionality of the product or system.

Reverse engineering can be a valuable tool for understanding how products and systems work, identifying potential issues, and improving upon existing designs. However, it is important to note that reverse engineering may be subject to legal restrictions, particularly in cases where intellectual property rights are involved.

In conclusion, reverse engineering is a valuable practice that can provide insights into the design and functionality of products and systems. By following a systematic approach and using the right tools, engineers can gain a better understanding of how products work and improve upon their designs.

# Chapter 32: Creating Malware with Python

Creating malware with Python can be a controversial topic, as it involves developing software that is intended to cause harm or disrupt computer systems. While it is important to be aware of the ethical considerations surrounding malware development, understanding how malware is created can also be beneficial for cybersecurity professionals looking to defend against such threats.

In this article, we will explore the process of creating malware with Python, including the different types of malware that can be developed, the tools and techniques used in the process, and the potential risks and consequences of engaging in malware development.

Types of Malware

Malware, short for malicious software, is a broad category of software that is designed to disrupt, damage, or gain unauthorized access to computer systems. There are many different types of malware, each with its own unique characteristics and methods of operation. Some common types of malware include:

Viruses: Viruses are programs that replicate themselves by infecting other files on a computer system. They can be spread through email attachments, infected websites, or removable storage devices.

Worms: Worms are self-replicating programs that spread

across computer networks, often exploiting vulnerabilities in software to infect other systems.

Trojans: Trojans are programs that appear to be legitimate software but actually contain malicious code that can harm a computer system or steal sensitive information.

Ransomware: Ransomware is a type of malware that encrypts a user's files and demands a ransom in exchange for the decryption key.

Spyware: Spyware is software that secretly gathers information about a user's activities on a computer system, often for the purpose of stealing sensitive information.

Tools and Techniques

Python is a popular programming language for malware development due to its versatility, ease of use, and extensive library of modules that can be used to create sophisticated malware. Some common tools and techniques used in creating malware with Python include:

Code obfuscation: Obfuscation techniques can be used to hide the true purpose of malware code and make it more difficult for antivirus software to detect.

Remote access: Python can be used to create malware that provides remote access to a compromised system, allowing an attacker to control the system from a remote location.

Keylogging: Keyloggers are a type of malware that records a user's keystrokes, allowing an attacker to capture sensitive information such as passwords and credit card numbers.

File encryption: Python can be used to create ransomware that encrypts a user's files and demands a ransom in exchange for the decryption key.

Network scanning: Python can be used to create malware that scans a network for vulnerable systems and exploits security weaknesses to gain unauthorized access.

Risks and Consequences

Creating malware with Python can have serious legal and ethical consequences, as it is illegal to develop or distribute software that is intended to cause harm or disrupt computer systems. Engaging in malware development can also expose individuals to criminal charges, civil lawsuits, and reputational damage.

Furthermore, malware can have a wide range of negative impacts on individuals, businesses, and organizations, including financial loss, data theft, and damage to reputation. Malware can also be used as a tool for espionage, sabotage, and cyber warfare, posing a threat to national security and public safety.

It is important for cybersecurity professionals to be aware of the risks and consequences of malware development and to focus on defending against malware threats rather than creating them. By understanding how malware is created and how it operates, cybersecurity professionals can better protect computer systems and networks from malicious attacks.

Conclusion

Creating malware with Python is a complex and controversial topic that raises important ethical and legal considerations. While understanding how malware is developed can be beneficial for cybersecurity professionals looking to defend against such threats, it is essential to approach this topic with caution and respect for the potential risks and consequences involved.

By focusing on defending against malware threats rather than creating them, cybersecurity professionals can help protect computer systems and networks from malicious attacks and contribute to a safer and more secure digital environment. It is important to stay informed about the latest trends and developments in malware and cybersecurity and to adhere to ethical standards and best practices in all aspects of information security.

# Chapter 33: Evading Detection and Forensics

In today's digital age, evading detection and forensics has become a critical skill for individuals and organizations looking to protect their privacy and security. Whether you are a journalist trying to protect your sources, a whistleblower exposing corruption, or a cybersecurity professional defending against cyber attacks, knowing how to evade detection and forensic analysis is essential.

There are various techniques and tools that can be used to evade detection and forensic analysis, ranging from simple encryption methods to more advanced tactics such as steganography and anti-forensic tools. In this article, we will explore some of the most effective strategies for evading detection and forensic analysis, as well as the potential risks and consequences of using these methods.

One of the most basic yet effective ways to evade detection is through encryption. By encrypting your communications and files, you can prevent unauthorized access and surveillance by third parties. There are various encryption tools available, such as PGP (Pretty Good Privacy) and VeraCrypt, that can be used to secure your data and communications.

Another technique for evading detection is steganography, which involves hiding secret messages or files within other files or images. By embedding sensitive information within seemingly innocuous files, you can avoid detection by automated scanning tools and human eyes. Steganography tools such as OpenStego and Steghide can be used to conceal your data in plain sight.

In addition to encryption and steganography, there are also anti-forensic tools that can be used to cover your tracks and erase digital footprints. Tools such as Tails OS and Whonix provide anonymous browsing and communication capabilities, making it difficult for adversaries to trace your online activities. By using these tools, you can evade detection and protect your privacy while browsing the internet.

However, it is important to note that evading detection and forensic analysis is not without risks. Using encryption, steganography, and anti-forensic tools may raise suspicions and attract unwanted attention from authorities or adversaries. In some jurisdictions, the use of these tools may even be illegal or subject to prosecution.

Furthermore, evading detection and forensic analysis may not always be foolproof. Advanced adversaries with sophisticated tools and techniques may still be able to uncover your activities and trace your digital footprint. Therefore, it is important to use these techniques in conjunction with other security measures, such as strong passwords, two-factor authentication, and regular software updates.

In conclusion, evading detection and forensic analysis is a critical skill for individuals and organizations looking to protect their privacy and security in today's digital age. By using encryption, steganography, and anti-forensic tools, you can secure your data and communications from unauthorized access and surveillance. However, it is important to weigh the risks and consequences of using these techniques, as well as to use them in conjunction with other security measures to maximize your protection.

# Conclusion

Congratulations on reaching the end of "Python for Web Hackers: Mastering Black Hat Techniques"! Throughout this journey, we've delved deep into the world of web hacking, exploring the intricacies and potential of Python to exploit and secure web applications.

From the outset, we immersed ourselves in the fundamentals of web vulnerabilities, starting with the notorious SQL injection and progressing through the complexities of cross-site scripting (XSS). We've dissected each type of attack, understanding their mechanics and learning how to craft powerful Python scripts to automate and enhance these exploits. Our exploration didn't stop there—we also uncovered advanced techniques to exploit lesser-known vulnerabilities, reinforcing the versatility and potency of Python in the hands of a skilled hacker.

The knowledge you've gained here is not just theoretical but immensely practical. You now have the tools to uncover and exploit vulnerabilities, demonstrating how attackers think and operate. By mastering these black hat techniques, you've also equipped yourself with the insights necessary to fortify defenses, making the digital world a safer place.

The true power of this book lies in the realization that security is a dynamic and ongoing process. The advanced scripts and automation techniques you've learned can not only penetrate but also protect, offering a dual perspective that is invaluable in today's ever-evolving cyber landscape.

As you move forward, remember that with great power comes great responsibility. The skills you've honed are powerful and must be wielded ethically and responsibly. Use your newfound expertise to challenge systems, uncover weaknesses, and contribute to a safer internet for all.

Thank you for embarking on this journey. Stay curious, stay vigilant, and continue to push the boundaries of what's possible with Python and web security. The world of ethical hacking is vast and ever-changing—may your path forward be filled with learning, growth, and impactful discoveries.

Happy hacking!

# Biography

**Jason Bourny** is a seasoned cybersecurity expert and a leading authority in the world of ethical hacking. With over a decade of hands-on experience in penetration testing and web application security, Jason has earned a reputation for his deep technical knowledge and innovative approaches to uncovering and mitigating vulnerabilities. His expertise spans the gamut of cybersecurity, from mastering Python for advanced hacking techniques to exploiting and securing web applications against the ever-evolving threats of the digital age.

Jason's passion for cybersecurity ignited early in his career when he realized the critical importance of protecting sensitive information and maintaining the integrity of web applications. This passion has driven him to not only become a proficient hacker but also a dedicated educator, committed to sharing his knowledge with aspiring security professionals and enthusiasts alike.

In addition to his professional pursuits, Jason is an avid hacker who thrives on the challenge of dissecting complex systems and finding creative solutions to security problems. He is deeply involved in the cybersecurity community, frequently contributing to open-source projects, participating in capture-the-flag (CTF) competitions, and sharing insights through blogs and speaking engagements.

When he's not immersed in the world of cyber defense and offensive security, Jason enjoys exploring the latest advancements in technology, honing his programming skills, and spending time with like-minded individuals who share his enthusiasm for making the digital world a safer place.

Jason's dedication to his craft, combined with his relentless curiosity and commitment to ethical hacking, makes him a true pioneer in the field. Through his book, "Python for Web Hackers: Mastering Black Hat Techniques," he aims to empower readers with the knowledge and skills needed to navigate and secure the complex landscape of web applications, inspiring a new generation of cybersecurity professionals to rise to the challenge..